1991
TRADITIONAL HOME™

In 1991 TRADITIONAL
HOME, we're proud to bring you a truly
magnificent collection of homes featured in the
pages of TRADITIONAL HOME™ magazine
during the past year. Through lavish photography
and well-written text, you'll visit homes whose
classic interiors typify the timeless beauty,
comfort, and livability we've come to associate
with traditional decor. These interiors reflect a
deep appreciation of our decorative heritage and
embrace a wide range of styles, including English
and French country, Victorian, American
colonial, and neotraditional design. Although
diverse in style, these homes share a common
bond: They all exhibit the unpretentious elegance
and self-assured character that are trademarks of
notable traditional interiors.

February

Linda Robertson loves all things romantic but
didn't want to overwhelm her husband and sons with
chintz and cranberry glass. Her gracious
Tulsa home is a harmony of feminine charm and
masculine comfort.

Through Rose-Colored Glasses

BY HEATHER WRIGHT

PHOTOGRAPHY BY GENE JOHNSON • PRODUCED BY NANCY E. INGRAM

A *faux-painted Louis XIV desk,* right, *showcases
a few of Linda's favorite things. Linda,* top, *sits at her desk with
Sadie, the Robertson family's King Charles spaniel.*

6

I think cranberry glass is my favorite collectible," muses Linda Robertson of Tulsa. "But I also love sterling silver, Staffordshire, porcelain boxes, Victorian beadwork, and majolica."

Linda's dream house would be an extension of her living room: swathed from floor to ceiling in soft color, floral fabrics, and filtered sunlight—a shrine to all things romantic; a serene place to showcase her pretty and delicate treasures.

"But I am definitely outnumbered," laughs Linda, who shares her home with three men: husband Clio, a doctor, and sons Chase, 11, and Adam, 8, *left.* "So when I decorated this house, I was careful not to let it become too feminine out of consideration for them."

Set against rolling green, bright azaleas, blooming dogwoods, and tall oaks, the Robertson residence is a rambling clapboard and brick house built sometime during the '40s but enlarged several times before they moved in three years ago. A friend of the family jokingly referred to the architecture as "pure Ozzie and Harriet," but inside the front door, the Nelsons

*T*reasures abound throughout the Robertsons' home, especially in the living room, above *and* opposite. Here, painted folding screens created by Linda's sister serve as a doorway to the dining room. The iron and glass coffee table is the room's sole contemporary accent. A 19th-century portrait of a young boy, opposite, commingles with snuff bottles, cranberry glass, and an antique bronze statuette. The room is resonant with a formal femininity.

would be dumbstruck. There, the Robertsons' home is "pure magic."

Together with Charles Faudree, a longtime friend and one of Tulsa's most prominent interior designers, Linda created an elegantly eclectic environment that is at once French and English, formal and casual, feminine and masculine.

The two mapped a strategy for making the house comfortable for everyone while still using Linda's many collections as a primary focus. "We were able to use almost all of the furniture from their previous home," Faudree recalls. "We recovered many things and gave old pieces new assignments in different rooms." And throughout the house, they reveled in something Faudree calls "disguise and deceit." With a little paint and fabric,

I wanted Clio to love collecting as much as I did, so I bought him a Napoléon letter opener hoping it would spark an interest. It did! Now he likes to go antique hunting too. Just look at his study. . . ."

—— LINDA ROBERTSON

C*lio Robertson's richly paneled study,* above, *is replete with Empire furnishings and Napoléon memorabilia, including a bronze bust, an oil portrait, epaulets, medals, and custom-made pillows with military flourishes. A French soldier's tin box and boots sit by the fireplace. The Empire daybed,* left, *and a tole table painted with a battle scene complete the rich effect of Dr. Robertson's masculine retreat.*

*T*he porch is our morning room,"
*Linda says. A bouquet of fresh color provided by
green wicker, bright floral chintz, a yellow
heirloom quilt, and a striped rag rug makes the
room seem part of the lush garden beyond.*

treasures emerged from pieces that were, in the beginning, quite ordinary. The living room provides two examples of a cunning use of paint: The mantel only appears to be a richly veined pink-and-green marble; and nondescript folding screens became striking works of art after Linda's sister transformed them into romantic panels of birds at play with ribbons.

The mantel and folding screens provide focal points in what Linda calls "the most formal and the most feminine room in the house." The living room's muted colors, floral fabrics, and fine French antiques provide a fitting backdrop to showcase Linda's collections of cranberry glass, porcelain boxes, snuff bottles, silver match safes, and 19th-century needlepoint—all

kept well within arm's reach of her two young sons. "Even when my boys were little, I kept things out so they would learn to appreciate and respect fine antiques," Linda says. "So far, it's been a success. Very few things have been broken."

Linda's love of antiques has long since caught hold of her husband. "When we were first married, I wanted Clio to love collecting as much as I did, so I bought him a Napoléon letter opener," Linda recalls. It worked like a charm. Clio Robertson's richly paneled study is testament to the fact that collecting can be *very* contagious. The room is brimming with elegant Empire furnishings and unusual French Revolution collectibles that Clio and Linda have found here and abroad.

14

*U*ntil a few years ago, the family room, right, was a garage. Its
rustic beams were salvaged from an old Kentucky farmhouse. The Dutch shipping
trunk next to the door was Linda's first antique purchase, at age 19.
"It cost $90—I thought that was a fortune!" The 19th-century English wardrobe,
below, cleverly conceals the television and stereo equipment.

*S*omeone once
told me to trust my
instincts—that if
I loved something, it
would work. I love
combining styles, so this
is a very eclectic house.
But it works."

—— LINDA ROBERTSON

Throughout the rest of the house—the
breakfast room, kitchen, family room, and
sun porch—Linda was adamant about
creating a comfortable environment for
her children but still hoped for a strong
undercurrent of elegance. Faudree knew
just what she meant. By mixing Linda's
English and French antique furniture free-
ly with brighter and warmer hues, eye-
catching texture, and well chosen
accessories, the two fashioned an eclectic,
sophisticated brand of informality.

The mood of the Robertsons' house
works well for the boys and is perfect for
the many black-tie dinners, Sunday
brunches, and other formal gatherings
Linda and Clio host each year. "We wanted the house to be very inviting but still
very elegant," Faudree says, adding with a
smile: "I think we achieved our goal." □

16

In love with the exuberant style of Victorian houses, antiques dealers Joe Christopher and Howard Siegel bought their Nyack, New York, home sight unseen when it went on the market for the first time in 180 years. Some surprises and a poignant tale of lost love came with the keys.

Victorian Icing
ON A FEDERAL CAKE

BY CARLA BREER HOWARD

PHOTOGRAPHY BY BILL STITES • PRODUCED BY BONNIE MAHARAM

The home's Victorian facade, above, *veiled the original simplicity of the structure.*

❦

Howard Siegel (standing) and Joe Christopher, left, *became avid gardeners after adding a greenhouse to their antiques shop, Christopher's. Here, they're relaxing on the porch with their dog, Nanette.*

❦

Rich in detail, the living room at right *is furnished in the opulent American rococo revival style. The interior harmonizes at last with the house's Victorian exterior.*

 uppose you had longed for years to own a particularly grand but neglected home in your area. Every time you drove by, your mind's eye would see the house's dark windows scrubbed clean and draped with soft silk. You imagined the exterior wonderfully repainted, a proud new porch at the front, the trees trimmed out back, flowers everywhere.

Howard Siegel and Joe Christopher, antiques dealers and avid collectors, also dreamed of redoing such a house. But whenever they drove by to look at the Victorian-style property they wanted, the real estate agents told them their dreams were hopeless. It would never be for sale. One family had hung on to the house since it was built in 1800.

Nevertheless, Joe and

Howard longed to enjoy the luxury of space and visual excitement afforded by a Victorian home, *this* home. So they went about the business of buying and selling antiques and waited patiently.

Then, amazingly, the landmark came up for sale. Howard and Joe didn't hesitate. Without stepping one foot inside, they bought the house.

Only half facetiously described by locals in this small, artistic community on the Hudson as "the haunted house," the property presented quite a challenge.

As Joe and Howard cautiously climbed the creaking front steps for the first time, doubts set in. Had they been a little hasty? After all, the condition of the house and the strange story of its occupant were local legend.

In the living room above, *the velvet-covered settee provides a pleasant place to enjoy hot chocolate. The cherished French cocoa set once belonged to Howard's mother. Nearby, a pair of sculptures composed of marble balls, each precariously balanced at the pinnacle of a rock, came from China.*

A living room tabletop, right, *holds examples of several of Howard and Joe's numerous collections. Particularly notable are the clear crystal paperweights and the whimsical bronze depicting an Oriental rug seller. The antique Italian vase is part of a larger collection. The soft rose moiré-covered walls make a lovely backdrop for the ornamental Victorian picture frames.*

"We expected to replace the porches, which had rotted and collapsed, the front steps, the electricity, and the plumbing," Howard notes, "but we weren't prepared for what we found when we opened the door and went inside." The house was a complete derelict.

Further, the outside of the home was ornately Victorian, but the inside was severely Federal. Why the strange contradiction in styles? Howard and Joe received some old photos of the house. From these, and a little research, they discovered that the house was originally built in 1800 in the Federal style so prevalent at the time. By no means designed as an imposing residence, the house very simply provided four square rooms placed over four square rooms. It was, as Howard and Joe describe it with some distaste, "as plain as it could be!"

Apparently the owner of the house in 1860 agreed. That year a local architect was engaged to grandly "Victorianize" the house, a common custom at the time. Evidently inspired, the architect obliged by adding the third floor, the tower with its ornamental wood shingles, the portico, and the front porch. Aptly, Howard calls the explosion of gingerbread a "Federal cake with Victorian icing."

However, left untouched by the remodel, the interior remained rigidly Federal. For two people who, according to Joe, "love the exuberance of Victorian houses," the inside

A prized piece in the living room, above, *the small Austrian walnut desk dates from the 1870s. The richly detailed pendulum of a Morbier clock hangs above the desk. Made in the early 1900s, the American dining room table and chairs at* right *are carved in the North Wind design. Howard's collection of frogs for holding flowers is reflected in the mirror over the mantel.*

A
Miss Havisham
Story

In the years before Joe Christopher and Howard Siegel bought the house, everyone knew it wasn't truly haunted. But with the yellowed shades always lowered, neighborhood stories abounded.

It was known, for instance, that the elderly lady concealed within was born and raised in the house that had been held by her family since 1800.

As a little girl, she would have played, skipped and daydreamed under the trees in that once-glorious garden.

Grown up, she was by all accounts a considerable beauty. Even so, she never married. Her father resolutely disapproved of the man she loved.

Bending to her father's will, she stayed at home. There she became a recluse, perhaps knowing too well how age can disappoint the lovely dreams of youth.

23

rooms were a big letdown.

After a Halloween haunted-house party (when costumed guests came accessorized with sledgehammers), the rebuilding process began.

Right away Howard and Joe discovered that 120 years after the Victorian remodel, nearly all of the wonderful wood gingerbread on the house's exterior was rotted and had to be replaced.

Inside, the damaged interior moldings were found to be plaster instead of wood. This meant replastering to build up the trim as well as to repair the ceilings.

Sealed off with cement, the fireplaces were reopened and the chimneys were relined. The lustrous white marble mantelpieces were revealed from beneath layers of black paint after hours of elbow-

pinching scraping.

Further, the house's electrical conversion, done four years previously, was faulty and desperately needed replacing.

All this completed, Howard and Joe could finally begin decorating the house. Although their shop specializes in country pine antiques, both Joe and Howard wanted another style of furniture to grace their own home. "After seeing one kind of furnishings all day,"

Joe and Howard fitted a sink into a 19th-century Austrian commode for their powder room at left by cutting into the existing marble top. The linen-fold motif on the drawer front is elegantly matched by the pleated chintz on the wall.

❧

The kitchen at right occupies a large sunny area made from two second-floor bedrooms. Rustic Mexican tile attractively complements the heavy chestnut worktable, which was once used in a Connecticut store.

❧

Howard and Joe's collection of mirrors, begun more than 16 years ago, illuminates the third-floor hall below. The Depression-era frames were whittled from cigar boxes.

Joe explained, "we wanted to see something different when we got home."

American rococo revival style, with its dark, richly carved wood and undulating forms, offered the perfect visual relief. In fact, this furniture provides the very essence of the Victorian charm Joe and Howard wanted for their home.

Now complete, the house resonates with a style of gracious hospitality its elaborate facade promised so many years ago. Both Joe and Howard like to cook and typically host dinner when entertaining friends. After being welcomed in the living room with drinks, guests move upstairs to the dining room. In warmer weather, they sit out on the porch and savor the shimmering view of the Hudson through the

porch's "moon gate."

For their overnight guests, Howard and Joe put the final touches on the tower guest room last summer. This was the last of an extraordinary decade-long effort. When asked if bringing this Victorian/Federal beauty back to its original splendor was worthwhile, Joe didn't hesitate to answer. "Let's put it this way, I get a thrill every night when I walk up the driveway. I love looking at this big pile of a house!" □

The old fieldstone scattered through the informal English-style gardens, left, adds a timeless texture to the landscape around a small pond.

❧

With a house full of fine collectibles, setting a memorable table on the front porch, right, is easy. The 19th-century American amber glasses give a golden glow against the brightness of the Battenberg lace linens and Grand Baroque flatware Howard inherited from his mother.

❧

The circular opening, or "moon gate," on the front porch below beautifully frames the view of the Hudson River in the distance.

Interior designer Harriet Robinson ensembled a
rich mosaic of old-world styles in her Midwest home and
created a gentle, yet continental, ambience throughout.

QUIET DRAMA

BY NANCY A. FANDEL

PHOTOGRAPHY BY JESSIE WALKER • INTERIOR DESIGN BY HARRIET ROBINSON

The house that interior designer Harriet Robinson and husband Marvin share is a simple ranch with clean, contemporary lines. Within, however, Harriet has cast an old-world spell. She's filled the home with precious gatherings from every century, from all over the world, by adding her own special touch of drama to the Robinsons' lives.

Harriet was raised in the Midwest by a mother who cared a great deal about her surroundings and having beautiful things. "My mother entertained with great style and dignity, and my father was extremely proud of her ability," says Harriet. "Though she was not directly educated in design, Mother was always creating. I guess it carried over to my sister and me. We both developed an intense interest in art and the culture around us."

That interest spurred Harriet on to study painting seriously for most of her academic life, and from that a talent grew that reached beyond her mother's

A quiet ranch-style facade, above right, *belies the international flair found inside the home of Harriet and Marvin Robinson. In the living room,* above, *Harriet's love of antiques is evident. The screen over the sofa is an American antique, a hand-colored lithograph on canvas from the Arts and Crafts Movement.*

29

inherent gifts. Slowly, through study, travel, and experience, Harriet developed her own innate ability to, as she says, "*feel* color and composition." Harriet's well-defined sense of color and knowledge of art are reflected in her work as an interior designer, and especially in her home.

The elements brought together by Harriet in her home range from warm-colored antique textiles and furniture to country-style charcoal-gray-and-white tile with terra-cotta inlays; from Indian wood carvings to cool-blue Persian vases; from Early American watercolors to Southeast Asian baskets.

The overall effect is a rich mosaic of traditional styles from diverse countries and continents. "I spend a great deal of time in England, France, and Italy," says Harriet. "One of my favorite sources for truly beautiful objects and antiques is in Venice, but England and France are the two countries that have had the greatest influence on my taste."

A walk through Harriet's home transports one to these other countries, other eras. The furnishings are classically oriented, similar in form and ornamentation. Rooms are graced with every European and Asian antiquity imaginable, all set against a backdrop of earth-tone walls and woodwork. An elegant continental ambience runs throughout, a feeling of warmth and friendliness amid the splendor. "I guess you could say I like things that are somewhat

To create warmth in the living room, above, *Harriet blended Italian silk velvet pillows with overstuffed furniture and a burled 19th-century Swedish chair with crowns on the arm posts. Her collection of Argentinean gourds,* left, *sits atop an English table hand-painted with designs that imitate inlaid marble, stone, and gilt.*

I PREFER DEEP, GRAYED-OUT
TONES WITH DEPTH AND CHARACTER TO FORM A
BEAUTIFUL BACKGROUND FOR ANTIQUES.

—— HARRIET ROBINSON

A 19th-century Aubusson rug with its autumn tones served as the basis for the color design in the dining room, right. A faux-marble painted wall treatment in creamy tones provides the perfect backdrop for Harriet's antiques. The valance above the window features an antique fabric of golds and rusts with cornucopias of flowers. The table—a family heirloom—showcases an antique Asian wedding sarong runner embroidered with gold. Empire chairs, covered in cream-colored silk velvet with silk voile backs, complete the warm color scheme of the room.

dramatic but not in a contrived way," says Harriet.

"It's also important to create intimate areas for a feeling of warmth," Harriet says. This philosophy is apparent in the Robinsons' living room. There, Harriet has designed many a cozy corner. In one, an art deco floor lamp casts a golden glow on an over-stuffed English settee with tapestry-covered pillows, inviting one to an evening of quiet reading or conversation. Overall, taupe and ivory walls and woodwork "create a warm and muted background for the antique textiles and furnishings in the room," says Harriet. "I didn't want the background to be in conflict with these beautiful pieces, but instead to add warmth, depth, and character."

As an interior designer, Harriet is always looking for just the right accessory, fabric, or antique to provide a sense of personal intimacy to her home and her clients'. One way she accomplished this in her home is with pillows. Noted for her collection of antique textiles, tapestries, needlepoints, and silk braids, Harriet designs pillows of every shape and size imaginable. She feels that pillows made from these European and Asian textiles are the most elegant of accessories. "They lend beauty and depth to each room," says Harriet.

Accessorizing doesn't need to take years, according to Harriet, but it's "far better to wait until you can add those things that truly enhance the beauty of a room rather than make the mistake of choosing items that may detract," she says.

The guest bedroom, above and left, reflects Harriet's discerning eye. Terra-cotta-colored walls and draperies made of stage-curtain-weight velvet balance the bearing and elegance of an English mahogany secretary with inlaid marquetry. Antique prints on the wall next to the secretary provide a counterpoint to the folk art.

A HOME SHOULDN'T LOOK LIKE AN ART
GALLERY. IT'S IMPORTANT TO CREATE INTIMATE
AREAS FOR A FEELING OF WARMTH.

—— HARRIET ROBINSON

Such was the case in the Robinsons' guest bedroom, where heavy Amish quilts and verdure tapestry have been combined with white cotton Victorian bedspreads. When Harriet was finishing this room, she was analyzing what to do about the bedspreads.

"I tried ecru or beige bedspreads with the quilts," says Harriet. "It was fine, but I knew it was boring. The spreads weren't doing anything for the room. I was stuck." Then one day, she was carrying a white spread around the house and happened into the guest bedroom. "It was like a thunderbolt hit me," says Harriet. "I had never considered white, but it was exactly what the room needed. It came alive!"

Harriet's credo throughout the design process of any room came from one of her mentors while Harriet was studying painting. "*Feel* the composition, Harriet, *feel* it," was the cry. "Sometimes I forget the importance of feeling the composition and I intellectualize instead," says Harriet. But in the end, Harriet's heart and feelings win over her head. The quiet drama of her lovely home is evidence. □

The kitchen, above *and* below, *was designed around the Thonet bentwood chairs, a Thonet pedestal from the 1800s, and a painted country cupboard from northern Italy. Atop the cupboard are whimsical pieces from Harriet's folk art collection. The white and charcoal-gray tile with terra-cotta inserts accomplished the country look Harriet wanted.*

April

TRADITIONAL HOME

THE SECRET OF HIS EXCESS

For Tulsa interior designer Charles Faudree, too much is not enough. Combining precious antique furnishings and collections very liberally, he transformed a straightlaced saltbox into an elegantly serendipitous showcase.

BY HEATHER WRIGHT

PHOTOGRAPHY BY GENE JOHNSON • PRODUCED BY NANCY INGRAM

Charles Faudree, *top*, basks in the sun with his dogs, Chelsea, Mr. Tuffington, and Chloe. A 200-year-old saltbox may seem out of place in Oklahoma, *above*, but a prominent Tulsa couple who collected colonial furnishings reconstructed it in 1953 from all-original materials found throughout New England.

Formerly dark and stuffy, the low-ceilinged keeping room, *left,* opened up after Charles pickled the woodwork and painted the walls pale yellow. Charles' passion for detail is apparent here, as is his love of dogs. Meissen pugs stand guard on a table and whippets colonize an 18th-century corner cupboard. The custom lamp, *below,* was fashioned from antique Staffordshire.

As an interior designer, Charles Faudree understands the dictum "less is more," but he doesn't pay homage to it. Quite the contrary. "For me, too much is not enough," he declares with a winsome smile. "I like overscale and overfurnishing. The more furniture there is in a room, the larger it appears."

This Tulsa-based designer's mantra of excess is not confined to just furniture, however. Charles also believes in dousing the home with accessories and personal collections. "They are every bit as vital to the end result," he says. "They're the frosting on the cake."

Personality runs rampant in Charles' design. Collections, he says, are vital to achieving this coveted but elusive effect.

Though this approach may conjure images of gauche and contemptible clutter, the reality of the homes Charles has fashioned is very different. The common thread throughout his work is a harmonious, albeit abundant, European sensibility that is at once cottage fresh and city smart.

41

The well-appointed living room, left, emanates continental grandeur. A French fruitwood commode, above, kennels many of Charles' cherished dogs along with other eclectic treasures. The 18th-century oil portrait of a boy and his dog was discovered at a Paris flea market. Tortoiseshell treasures, below, gleam in the shelves and upon the drop front of a black-and-gold lacquered secretary that opens to reveal a scarlet japanned interior. "Go for a surprise now and then," Charles suggests.

In the master bedroom, *right,* rich texture, neutral tones, lively pattern, and gold flourishes create a mood reminiscent of an English gentleman's study. "I love every room in the house," Charles says, "but when we're alone, and the weather keeps us in, you can usually find the dogs and me curled up in here." The French powder bath, *below,* is period furnishing at its finest.

Though Charles' own home represents the purest distillation of his design principles, this wasn't easily achieved. The house that he bought three years ago was a true New England saltbox, the realities of which were small rooms, claustrophobic ceilings, and a puritanical rigidity that are all in direct opposition to Charles' great fondness for French splendor and English comfort.

Charles adores the decorating of the design process. "I love creating tablescapes," he says. "For me, it's exhilarating."

It was, however, a design challenge he couldn't resist. "It was a purist's colonial," he recalls. "Everything about it was seventeenth- or eighteenth-century American. At first I shuddered at the thought of disturbing it, but it was now my house, and I was determined to make it *my* home."

The colonial palette was the first thing to go. In its place, bright colors gave the stark rooms a new vitality. Crisp floral, striped, and fruit motifs on upholstery and draperies

A recent addition to the original saltbox, the great-room, *left,* has a light, informal, even somewhat contemporary mood. The vaulted roof, a modern stone chimney, and modest mattress ticking upholstery provide fresh counterpoint to distressed oak, English blue-and-white china, and a delicate French birdcage. The new kitchen, *below,* adjoins the great-room. "My guests always congregate here," Charles says, "and when the weather's right, the party usually spills out onto the terrace," *above.*

imbued the common rooms with warmth reminiscent of an English cottage in Cotswold, Charles' favorite region.

Drawing upon the resources of his own antiques and design store, Charles arranged and rearranged his European furnishings. "It's not easy," he says. "You have to play with it, give your eye rest, then come back to it again."

And after his furniture was finally in place, Charles began combining accessories and personal collections to create tablescapes. "It's the part I love best," he says. "It's just exhilarating."

A guest room, *left,* doubles as a showcase for Charles' Napoléon memorabilia, which includes statuary, portraits, medals, and other regalia. Charles disassembled a French daybed to make caned headboards for the room's two twin beds. An adjoining guest bath, *below,* perpetuates the mood with bibelots, opulent fabric-upholstered walls, and a sink crafted from a campaign chest.

Each room contains at least a handful of Charles' bountiful and engaging tablescapes, which double as showcases for bright caches of his eclectic collections. Throughout the house, Staffordshire, Meissen, English blue-and-white porcelains, tortoiseshell, antique birdcages, Napoléon memorabilia, and all manner of ornament depicting dogs mingle with wit and grace.

"Collecting is a disease," he says, laughing. "You buy the first piece because you love it, but from there it becomes a craziness."

Charles Faudree may genially profess that "too much is not enough," but his home says something else entirely: Here is a man who knows there is a world of difference between opulent abundance and oppressive clutter. What *is* the secret of his excess? "It's a fine line," Charles says modestly, "one I always walk cautiously and with my glasses on straight." □

Charles has collected Napoléon regalia for 20 years. His sentimental favorite? The first little print he ever bought.

The DOOR Is Always Open

BY NANCY A. FANDEL
AND CARLA BREER HOWARD

PHOTOGRAPHY BY RICK TAYLOR
PRODUCED BY RUTH L. REITER

Triumphant over the ravages of Hurricane Hugo last autumn, the Charleston-area historic home of Joan and Don Brown continues its proud tradition of hospitality.

From their waterside home, the Brown family, *above, enjoys the activity in Charleston Harbor. Clockwise from left: daughter Shannon holding her rabbit; Jodi with an arm around her dad, Don; Deedee; Joan; and Bo.*

An old wicker baby buggy on the sun porch, *left, is part of Joan's collection of Wakefield and Bar Harbour pieces. The antique ice cream parlor chairs add to the nostalgic setting for a family Sunday brunch.*

The Browns' home, *right, rests on a quiet street in the village of Mount Pleasant, South Carolina. Known for years as The Harbour House, it was built as a summer residence in the 1840s.*

The Door Is Always Open

I t's all right. Really. Just walk up to the door and knock. Don or Joan Brown or one of their four children will welcome you warmly into their charming world of white lace, Old English chintz, and refined comfort. "We have a casual life and don't know who's going to drop in," says Joan. "I want a good feeling when they walk in the door."

And a good feeling is just what you'll get. Expect to be treated like one of the family. There's a laid-back, familiar life-style here in Mount Pleasant, South Carolina, once a summer escape for residents of neighboring Charleston. The aura of those sleepy days gone by still lingers, and the Browns like it that way.

As you enter the Brown home, the living room—a real *living* room, says Joan—sets the tone for a home where charm and elegance are surpassed only by comfort. Over-stuffed botanical print chairs and sofas—skirted and gently grazing the antique Heriz rug—mix well with a flame-stitch wing chair and rose-colored love seat. Snuggle

The fine English chintz fabric in the living room, above, blends well with the antique Heriz on the pine floor. The picture above the fireplace depicting the Browns' home was painted by a friend of Joan's, Shirley Kratz.

Joan chose simple window treatments for the living room, right, to emphasize the views. A portrait of son Bo hangs over the game table. The armoire in the corner was originally used as a linen press.

The Door Is Always Open

Joan, Bo, and Shannon prepare lunch in the kitchen, above. The pine floor in this room is original. The pine-seated stools are from an ice cream parlor.

Creating a dramatic backdrop for her blue-and-white porcelain and mahogany furnishings, Joan chose red walls for the dining room, left. Antique chairs with Chinese-patterned seat covers carry the theme.

into that chair next to the fire, choose a book from the built-in shelves flanking the fireplace, and make yourself right at home.

Just off the living room is the glassed-in sun porch, where Joan and Don do most of their entertaining. The cozy main-level room is furnished with old wicker, a pine table covered with white lace and paired with old ice cream parlor chairs, and plants of every kind. A fern nestles neatly in an antique wicker baby buggy. Glassed doors lead back to the living room or to the dining room, kitchen, or an outside porch.

From every corner of this sun-streaked piazza, as well as from the bottom-level porch and top-floor master bedroom, the view is spectacular. A boardwalk stretches along the waterfront, protecting the home from changes in the tide. You can hear the shrimp boats whistle as they breeze by in the golden

The Door Is Always Open

glow of each day's dawning. Grab your wine. Joan's in the kitchen.

"Everyone hangs [out] in the kitchen," says Joan with a laugh. The warm-colored pine floor is original to the house. A friend, Shirley Kratz, painted scenes of Mount Pleasant and Charleston on some of the tiles on the center island and counter-tops. A border of flowers has been stenciled onto the white walls.

After you retire to the main-floor guest room, Don and Joan climb the stairs to their private retreat on the top level. Former-ly the attic, this peaked-ceiling room is an ideal backdrop for the four-poster the couple has shared since the early days of marriage. A wall separates the sleeping area from a sitting room—a favorite spot to enjoy

an after-dinner coffee as the night grows cool and the house becomes quiet.

You'll find it is peaceful at night. A fog-horn moos in the distance. The lights of Charleston sparkle across the water like stars fallen from the South Carolina sky. You've shared the Browns' gentle southern life. □

The seating area in the master bedroom, left, *was furnished with comfort in mind. Don and Joan often enjoy late-night refreshments here.*

The Browns' master bedroom, above, *was once the home's attic. Now romance reigns as lovely lace covers a four-poster, and a rose-laden bedskirt drapes loosely onto mauve carpet.*

The bath, opposite, *accommodates guests and serves as the family's powder room. Refined touches such as lace curtains, an old chandelier, and beadboard paneling reflect the home's interior design.*

Joan's love of white lace is never more evident than in Jodi's room, left. *Jodi wears the paper white dress that appears in her portrait.*

Photograph: Bill Sites

When their dark and labyrinthine
1735 colonial started closing in on them,
Frank and Louise Cashman
tinkered with a historical design and built anew.
The result is a light and livable house
with 250-year-old roots.

THIS *New* HOUSE

BY DAN WEEKS

PHOTOGRAPHY BY JOHN JENSEN • PRODUCED BY BONNIE MAHARAM

The Cashmans' new house, above, has caused more than one passerby
to knock on the door and ask, "When was this built?" Inside, 18th- and
19th-century American antiques such as the Connecticut Queen
Anne table and chairs, right, bask in a corner of the light and spacious
living room afforded by this updated colonial design.

our years ago, Frank and Louise Cashman left their 1735 farmhouse and built a reproduction colonial next door. The new house, which they designed and decorated themselves, balances their reverence for the past with their desire for a spacious and comfortable home.

When the Cashmans inherited their old house from Frank's parents, they moved right in—to a museum. Frank's folks had spent a lifetime collecting Early American furniture. Each carefully arranged room was packed with antiques, and the house itself was preserved in nearly original condition. Bathrooms and appliances were hidden away. Even the daylight that filtered dimly through the house's tiny hand-blown panes seemed centuries old.

The house was so complete that Frank and Louise hesitated to make even the slightest change. The couple read and cooked by the flickering light of electrified candlesticks. They bought mostly antique toys for their sons, and hid the occasional Tonka truck beneath the dust ruffle of the boys' creaking bedsteads. Family photographs were kept in closed drawers, in deference to the many period paintings and daguerreotypes displayed on the walls.

Louise reminisces about life in the old house in the tones of someone awakened from a dream. "We kind of got carried away" with authenticity, she says.

Linen white walls offset the graceful dining room chairs, drop-leaf table, and cherry side table, opposite—*all circa 1730. The silk moiré window treatment picks up the soft tones of the wide pine flooring and Heriz rug. Colonial detailing includes beaded taupe trim and 12-over-12 double-hung windows. Black basalt coffee- and teapots,* above, *grace the side table. They belonged to Frank's parents' Wedgwood collection. An antique cupboard on the dining room wall,* below, *holds antique tea pitchers, spoons, and caddies.*

A *large window, light-colored fabrics and walls, and natural pine floor provide cheerful counterpoint to the living room's dark wood furniture. The wing chair, candlestand, and butterfly-top table date from the 1700s.*

The guest bedroom, opposite and below, is decorated sparingly, focusing attention on the personality of each piece. The 18th-century bed and its companion table are covered with reproduction Marseilles spreads from Portugal. On the table, pocket watches handed down through the Cashman family are displayed. Louise made the cut-paper lampshade herself. She also fashioned the rug, copying the pattern from the back of a wing chair in the Metropolitan Museum of Art. An English footstool, floral-pattern curtains, and a small floor rug add touches of color to the room.

Gradually, the Cashmans sensed that they had become hostages to the distant past. Beautiful as their inherited home was, they yearned to live in a place more hospitable to the life-style of a growing family.

They wanted a bright, light, and spacious home, one that combined the classic design and hand detailing they were used to, with the modern amenities they had forsworn. After much research, Frank and Louise created the new house that you see here.

It was an ambitious undertaking, but Frank has an architectural bent and Louise is an interior designer, so they were well suited to the task. Plus, says Louise, "When you build a reproduction you can tap into sources such as museums, manufacturers, and craftsmen specializing in reproductions that are very enthusiastic about helping you do it right." The exterior detailing—including the large center chimney, the 12-over-12 windows, and the 10-pitch cedar-shingled roof—was borrowed from an 18th-century house in Southbury, Connecticut. The entryway duplicates that of a house in historic Deerfield, Massachusetts.

The entry was built by a master craftsman to Louise's scale drawings. "If you're going to do something like this, you might as well pay attention to the details," says Louise. The doors are hand-pegged, hand-planed, and feature hand-blown bull's-eye glass in the lights. The house

*W*hen you build a reproduction you can tap into sources . . . that are very enthusiastic about helping you do it right. . . . If you're going to do something like this, you might as well pay attention to the details.

—— LOUISE CASHMAN

65

is set well back from the road and low to the ground, in the early manner. "When it weathers down," says Frank, "you won't be able to tell that it's a reproduction."

Inside, the Cashmans worked to team a spacious, efficient layout with the house's period features. "Combining an eight-foot-square center chimney with a center hall was tricky," says Louise, "but we were committed to an authentic facade." On the house's south-facing back side, they took a few design liberties: skylights and large thermopane windows (with snap-in muntins) flood the house with daylight.

Wide pine flooring, beaded trim, antique beams, and Rumford fireplaces—a shallow and efficient early design—carry the colonial feeling inside. Louise furnished the house with pieces from Frank's parents' collection. With a few exceptions, Louise chose the spare, graceful elegance of the collection's William-and-Mary furnishings.

Linen white walls and historic shades of taupe- and green-painted trim emphasize the spaciousness and clean design of the rooms, and focus attention on the beautiful furniture.

There is an ancient Chinese curse: "May all your wishes come true." If all wishes were as well conceived as the Cashmans' for a livable colonial, the curse would be a blessing.

"Living in this house is wonderful," says Frank. □

"A *big, cozy kitchen with a fireplace and a view," was the Cashmans' vision. The fireplace,* below, *is an authentic and efficient Rumford design surrounded by raised-panel detailing. Pewter candle holders and antique Canton plates decorate the mantel, while a wag-on-wall clock keeps time. Louise teamed a cherry breakfast table and reproduction chairs,* above, *with an antique hutch housing a pewter collection.*

June

TRADITIONAL HOME

Summer Always

Surrounded by June colors right out of a Fragonard canvas, a young Massachusetts family enjoys year-round brightness in its 1920s waterfront home.

BY CARLA BREER HOWARD

PHOTOGRAPHY BY D. RANDOLPH FOULDS
PRODUCED BY ESTELLE BOND GURALNICK

*Moving attention to detail enhances the charm of the living room **above**. The swag and jabot window treatment is lined in pale blue to match the ceiling color. The faux-painted mantel **right** cleverly depicts the homeowners' favorite hobbies in the manner of delft tiles.*

*The summery living room's peach crackle wallpaper, pale blue ceiling, and pickled floor, **above**, express the happy feeling the owners sought. A splash of favorite Cape Cod flowers scattered on a beige ground animates the carpet's design.*

...Cod has been an American tradition for ...rs. The clapboard homes that dot the rocky ...chusetts region testify to the summer ...et side by side so that all can afford a view ...ater. Windows turn toward the sea, ready to be thrown open to catch the cooling breezes.

Such were the characteristics of the home featured here. A vacation retreat built in the 1920s on a prime spot on Cape Cod, the waterfront property had spectacular views from every room and a wonderful traditional feeling.

Still simply a warm-weather house when the current homeowners found it, the structure needed complete winterizing, a new roof, windows and siding, and a heating system before it could become the year-round residence they wanted. For help with the eight-month-long task, the couple turned to Boston designer Richard FitzGerald.

As FitzGerald began, he discovered that the floor plan of the house was open and bright, but the original entrance was neatly tucked from view at the side of the house. "You couldn't find the front door," says FitzGerald. He suggested

*S*ituated high on a bluff of a small Cape Cod island, the house commands spectacular 270-degree views. For waterfront pleasures, a separate beach house and dock are just a few steps away, directly below on the bay.

*F*urnishings, flowering plants, and the glorious view give the porch **right** its considerable charm. A pair of flamboyantly designed armchairs, carved by a Maine craftsman in the 1930s, adds a note of fun to the inviting seating. A dining set (out of view) adds to the area's use as an outdoor living room.

A bountiful summer salad-and-herb garden, **left**, keeps the family table filled with fresh lettuce and cucumbers, as well as sweet tomatoes and peppers. With its raised beds, the garden is easily managed by the homeowners.

new French doors for the entry, surrounded by a brick facade for contrast to the clapboard siding. "They loved the idea, and we went ahead with it," he says.

Inside the front door, FitzGerald took out a second-floor bedroom over the foyer in order to create a soaring new entry hall that would complement the new entryway. "It was a minor change architecturally which made a major difference in the feel of the house," says FitzGerald. Now, from the moment one enters the home there is the airy feeling of a country summer's day. Wallpaper—chosen for its lovely colors of melon, periwinkle-blue, and green—is "an up-feeling documentary," says FitzGerald, depicting beautifully drawn flowers. It sets a bright, light tone for the house.

The goals for interior design were simple enough and read like a description of summer living. FitzGerald remembers casual elegance, comfort, and soft colors being key requests made by the homeowners. They wanted a house with a cheery atmosphere where they could put their feet up in any room.

*W*ith its delicately colored, faux-painted chairs and
fireplace mantel, the dining room **above** and **opposite** suggests
a New England country summer. The 19th-century
French dining table and the homeowners' pottery collection in
the nearby antique Welsh cupboard enhance that impression.

The living room coddles guests in two down-filled sofas and
a chaise longue for fireside relaxing. Another chaise-by-a-
fireplace arrangement creates comfort for the owners in their
master suite. Even the upright seating around the dining room
table is offset by comfortably upholstered pieces along the
walls. The soft draping of window treatments and subtly
textured rugs further give one the feeling of being cosseted.
"The feel in this living room is casually elegant, geared to a
young family that does a lot of entertaining," says FitzGerald.

He also brought the soft colors of Marie Antoinette's
favorite painter, Jean-Honoré Fragonard, to the home. The
blue on the living room ceiling mirrors the tone of a warm
afternoon sky painted long ago. The muted ivory background
of the living room carpet finds its counterpart in the creamy
mist of the artist's clouds. And the rosy-peach hue of the
chaise brings to mind the heated cheeks found on Fragonard's
frolicking cherubs.

Being a primary residence, the home was also given finishing
touches. Decorative painter James Smith was brought from
New York to work his special magic. He managed to

*I*n the kitchen,
new tile, a butternut ceiling,
country floral-print fabrics,
and a collection of
antique copper pots create a
gentle, welcoming
environment for the family.

73

*T*his truly seems to be
a happy house. It comes from the
people in it, the location,
and the sense of light throughout.
In fact, there's not a dark corner
in it anywhere.

—— RICHARD FITZGERALD

*S*itting on the terrace, shown at **right,** is one of the
family's greatest pleasures in the summertime. There, they take
their meals and watch the passing pageant of boats, water-
skiers, and fishermen. Beds of impatiens, a favorite of the
homeowners, edge the brick flooring in a frame of soft colors.

*R*eplacing an
awkward side door as the
main entrance, the new entry
left has double French
doors framed by new brick. A
matching extension to the
house's facade was added to
accommodate a new master
bedroom closet.

transform an otherwise straightforward mantelpiece in the living room into a gallery of delicately aged delft tiles. The tiles cleverly depict the family's favorite hobbies of boating, flower arranging, and golfing. The mantel in the dining room was also given a new personality when Smith faux-painted it to look like stone.

In the master bedroom, the painter created a softer look. He not only added graceful highlights and flourishes over the fireplace, but by applying a gentle ivory wash with deep green and gold accents, he rescued the owners' four-poster from being an overwhelming mahogany presence in the room.

FitzGerald responded to his clients' love of chintz, particularly in the living room. Seat cushions and pillows in delightful patterns play cheerfully against the dark rich woods of the room's fine antiques. The colorful florals in the living room and on the porch pillows—seen just outside through the French doors—complement the flower-filled gardens (see photo *above* and on *page 71*).

A pair of cushioned rocking chairs and a lazy swing draw the family to the open outside porch area. There, they can relax and take in the activity on the waterfront below. The porch faces northwest and overlooks the bay. They live out on the terrace in the summer, eating their meals and entertaining there. They can open the doors to the living room and dining room for an easy indoor/outdoor flow.

To others, it might be a bit difficult to imagine living year-round amid summer's colors and warmth on the shores of Massachusetts. The autumns there are gold and rust, after all; the winters blustery and cold. And though the spring holds the promise of clear skies and sunshine, rain presses against the windows without mercy most days.

But in this home, summer is with the family always; life is serene and soft. "The sun shines into the house all the time, from every room," says FitzGerald. "With four fireplaces and a beautiful view of the harbor, it's very cozy in the winter as well as the summer." □

*D*ecorative painter
James Smith embellished the
fireplace mantel in the
master bedroom **above** as
well as the mahogany
bed in light, creamy tones.
The homeowner and her
twin sister, **right**, often play
backgammon together.

A vibrant, documentary-inspired wallpaper energizes
the new entry hall **top**. The painted 18th-century Swedish clock
and antique French armchair are among the family's prized
pieces. The powder room's decor **above** takes its theme from the
serendipitous floating stars motif in the wallpaper.

77

Gypsy Colors

Drawn to intense colors since childhood, Virginia Burney chooses a bold palette for her Oregon home.

BY CARLA BREER HOWARD

PHOTOGRAPHY BY JOHN VAUGHAN • PRODUCED BY BARBARA MUNDALL
INTERIOR DESIGN BY VIRGINIA BURNEY

Virginia Burney and her husband, Dick Bach, **above,** *relax on their back porch. The front of the house* **right** *features a curved flagstone pathway and a wood porch where bold-color flowers set the stage for the home's dramatic interiors just inside the door.*

A tropical-inspired painting hangs over a pine chest, **opposite,** *in the dining room. Dick's grandmother carried the ornate silver candlestick with her when fleeing from Romania.*

The vivid colors of a Gypsy woman's shawl surround Virginia Burney. Drawn to bright reds, purples, and yellows since childhood, the Portland, Oregon, designer colors her home, garden—even her wardrobe—from a rich palette. "I've always liked intense colors," she says. "They make me feel good!"

First-time visitors to the home Virginia shares with her husband, Dick Bach, often are drawn from room to room, beguiled by the colors of the interiors. "People come in, stop in their tracks, and say, 'I'd really love to visit, but do you mind if I just look around a little bit first?'" muses Virginia. "It's hard to keep eye contact!"

At such moments Virginia remembers back to 1964, when, against everyone's advice, she bought this house. Then a single mother of two little boys, she stubbornly looked to the run-down structure's potential rather than its problems. "It was the worst house in the best neighborhood that I could almost afford," she says with a chuckle.

The task of rehabilitating the home was immense and her budget just the opposite. But, with a lot of elbow grease and perseverance, Virginia gradually renewed the home's appearance and stature within the well-kept neighborhood. When she painted the exterior of the home, which hadn't seen a new coat of paint for years, Virginia's appreciative neighbors threw her a party.

In the living room below, an undulating paisley pattern camouflages the size of a sectional sofa. Nubby handwoven pillows, the subtle glow of brass accessories, and an Afghan cradle turned into a coffee table lend an air of Oriental exoticism.

The living room fireplace right was surrounded with shiny corrugated tiles when Virginia moved in. She replaced them with a golden-veined Italian marble, creating immediate elegance.

A corner table in the living room left holds a collection of crystal and brass inkwells plus some prized pieces of old Imari. The lamp was fashioned from an Oriental vase Virginia found on one of her antiquing trips.

It was the worst house in the best neighborhood that I could almost afford. All my friends said no sensible person would buy it.

—— VIRGINIA BURNEY

*V*irginia selected the matte-finish dark blue wallpaper in the dining room **left** to set off her gilt-framed artwork and pine furnishings.

A gift of one Imari plate many years ago began the couple's collection of blue-and-white porcelain, displayed in the dining room **right**. Virginia regards her array of exotic pillows—such as those with the mirrored fabric from India—as extensions of her art collection.

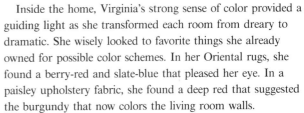

Inside the home, Virginia's strong sense of color provided a guiding light as she transformed each room from dreary to dramatic. She wisely looked to favorite things she already owned for possible color schemes. In her Oriental rugs, she found a berry-red and slate-blue that pleased her eye. In a paisley upholstery fabric, she found a deep red that suggested the burgundy that now colors the living room walls.

Recognizing that deep saturated tones can be overpowering when used in large quantities, Virginia tested several colors before making final choices. Painting various tones on sections of walls, she viewed them for a number of days and even polled other family members for their reaction before choosing the winning colors.

Throughout the home, Virginia used crisp white on the ceiling, woodwork, and shutters to provide visual relief from the deep colors of the walls and furnishings. Smaller touches of white, provided by lampshades and picture mats, also have a calming effect.

Someone else might have decided against dark colors because they typically can close up a space, making a room feel smaller than it actually is. Not Virginia. By choosing the same tone of red for the living room sectional sofa and the walls, she created a unified, space-enlarging

sweep from floor to ceiling. "A white couch wouldn't have worked," she says. "The contrast would have interrupted the eye and made the room seem smaller."

It's not surprising that Virginia's passion for deep, dark colors also surfaces in the accessories that embellish every room. Imari pottery, paintings (some old, others contemporary pieces done by northwestern artists), rugs, and fabrics are unified by their rich coloration. Virginia doesn't select her collectibles to match her rooms, however. Her choices are emotional—and lasting—ones. Even today she displays the pair of brightly painted ducks and an inlaid Oriental box she bought at the age of seven with ice cream money she'd saved. "Oddly enough, I still love them and that's still the kind of thing I would look for today," she says.

Virginia's favorite resting spot is the corner of the living room sofa. Her telephone, TV, music, magazines, and blanket are all within easy reach. On most days, in late afternoon, she settles back into the deep paisley cushions. Her Gypsy colors and treasured possessions are everywhere in view. From here she can gaze out through the back-porch French doors. Sunlight touches the bright red leaves of the Fotinia tree she planted just outside. At such moments Virginia smiles, delighting in the vividly colored world of her making. □

*P*illows from China, Japan, Guatemala, and India lend exoticism to the otherwise airy simplicity of wicker furnishings on the back porch **right**. *The family cat, Little Bit, spies something fun to chase in the tree.*

*T*he compact kitchen **above** *was fitted with roomier cabinetry selected to look original to the house. As an example of Virginia's carefully cultivated vistas of greenery, the kitchen doorway opens to a colorful container garden. This way, she can almost believe she lives in a forest.*

*T*he countertop vignette in the kitchen **left** *includes some favorite porcelains and a watercolor done by Virginia.*

From the
Ground Up

BY HEATHER WRIGHT

PHOTOGRAPHY BY RICK TAYLOR • PRODUCED BY EILEEN DEYMIER

*The colonial manor Janet Montgomery wanted wasn't for sale,
so she bought 18 acres of Maryland's rolling green and built
her own dramatic version on the 200-year-old model.*

S itting atop 18 well forested acres a comfortable distance from an old country road, Janet Montgomery's rural Maryland manor appears serenely colonial.

The stately brick and white clapboard house looks as though it was built before an American republic was

more than a twinkle in Tom Paine's eye. It emanates the dignity and grace of an old family home meticulously kept up and handed down with purpose from one generation to the next.

Because the sense of heritage here is so heady, the impression upon first entering Janet's home is momentarily disorienting: The great flood of sunlight and grand scale are about the last things you'd expect to find inside a 200-year-old colonial, as is the drama. A tall archway leading from the marbled foyer reveals a great-room with walls of glass soaring skyward. Welcome back to the late 20th century.

T*he foyer* above *makes a dramatic welcoming statement with its sweeping staircase and marble floors. The pedestal entry table was custom-made from an 18th-century epergne, acrylic, and glass.*

A *leviathan design challenge, the great-room* right *is 30×40 feet with 18-foot ceilings. Interior designer Suzé Jones began with an 80-year-old serape rug and added sectional sofas and a marbleized coffee table. Atop the table* left *is a sterling biscuit box that dates to the 17th century. A 12-foot-long breakfront behind the sofa suits the room's massive scale.*

> *"The timeless appeal of the architecture Janet chose for her home cried out for compatible interiors."*
>
> — SUZÉ SURDYK JONES

In the living room opposite as throughout the house, designer Jones kept the window treatments simple. She framed the window bar with tailored swags and jabots to let the sun stream in. Richly varied fabrics in the room enhance, rather than compete with, a bold tribal carpet.

Built-in shelving on each side of the dining room fireplace left was designed to showcase Janet's collection of Herend porcelain. A dressy stripe on the Chippendale dinner suite's chairs repeats hues found in the room's billowy balloon shades.

The table is set with Herend's Canton, below, a pattern first made in the 19th century and now custom-painted. Scarlet Fu dogs, also Herend, heighten the dinner's Oriental mood.

"That's exactly the effect I had in mind," Janet says of the house she built seven years ago. "I love the colonial look, but there were modern features I really wanted—especially wide open spaces and lots of light."

Originally, Janet had her heart set on a real Revolutionary War-era manor. Though she would drive by, day after day, to admire it, the owners simply weren't interested in selling. "I'd fallen in love with a house I couldn't have," she says. "When I finally came to terms with that, I began planning this house, which is, I think, neocolonial in the best sense of it."

Even before construction was complete, Janet enlisted interior designer Suzé Surdyk Jones to help her decorate her new "old" home. "I wanted it to be traditional," Janet explains, "but I also wanted drama and comfort."

As with the house itself, Janet and Jones designed each room from the ground up. Finding the right rugs and carpet was their first task. "We looked for examples that were warm, elegant and unique, but which all worked well together," Jones says.

"I wanted both drama and comfort in this house. I like surprise and impact but didn't want a showplace."

— JANET MONTGOMERY

An antique serape rug became the focal point in the great-room. Jones then built upon it with peach walls, white trim, neutral upholstery, and modern art in order to make the huge space warm and inviting.

Though the great-room flows naturally into the rest of the house, Janet and her designer shared a more frankly traditional vision for other rooms. Using Janet's favorite colors—blues, creams, and peaches—as her primary palette, Jones went about creating a living room, dining room, master bedroom suite, and study steeped in an elegant timelessness that mirrors the house's stately colonial facade.

"These rooms would have been appropriate twenty-five years ago," Janet says, "and it's a safe bet they still will be twenty-five years from now." Just like the house itself. □

Inviting floral armchairs and a matching pouf near the fireplace in Janet's bedroom above *create an intimate environment for into-the-night talks or for sipping orange juice while reading the Sunday paper. A chaise upholstered in a complementary plaid, a four-poster bed, and a ladies' secretary,* bottom left, *complete the master suite's cozy mood.*

The handsome library right *departs from the home's quiet palette. A cowhide chair and a vibrant rug make the paneled room anything but sedate.*

welcome call...

Lace and flowers add to the boudoir feeling in Gail and Edd Ghent's dining room, right. The mirror, with its Queen Anne lines, reflects ivy topiaries and a vase overflowing with colorful anemones.

Gail and Edd, below, share their St. Louis home with their two college-age children, their frisky pup, Rufus, and a tomcat named Phineas.

A PAINTERLY APPROACH

Gail Ghent dreamed for years of living in
the gracious world of an impressionist painting. Today,
her St. Louis home captures that fantasy.

BY SUSAN DAVIDSON

PHOTOGRAPHY BY WILLIAM N. HOPKINS • PRODUCED BY MARY ANNE THOMSON

*W*inslow Homer created a painting titled *Croquet Scene* in 1866. Three women stand, adorned in colorful taffetas. Their delicately gloved hands grasp mallets as they wait expectantly for courtly gentlemen to play the game. This soft and languorous life-style from the past is the one Gail Ghent has chosen to live today.

The front of the Ghent house right *has an old-world flavor. Delicate English roses ramble up the mailbox and onto the porch, where a neoclassical stone cherub beneath the colonnaded entrance shyly greets all visitors.*

Awash in late afternoon light, the dining table far right *is set with family silver and white porcelain chargers inset with vibrant majolica dinner plates. Lace swags nipped with blue satin bows grace the windows.*

The birdhouses below *belonged to Edd's great-aunt Hazel, who was said to be legendary for her love of birds.*

"I always wanted to be a lady in that painting," Gail says with delight. "I don't want to just paint, I want to live in an impressionist painting."

Art and nature are Gail's twin passions. She loves the incandescent open-air paintings of Monet and the opulent Victorian indolence of John Singer Sargent: Within their canvases, life is refined, sublime. It is this world Gail has captured in her St. Louis home—a charming, English-style cottage at the end of a lane overgrown with glossy hollies.

Gail, a longtime antiques dealer, and her husband, Edd, who works for McDonnell Douglas Corp., raised two children in a traditional white colonial filled with American country antiques. Although the country pieces were lovely to behold, they elicited a more rustic approach to life's comforts than what Gail longed for.

*The living room display cabinet above left was painted
by Gail in plum and green to highlight her
collection of majolica. A cherub swathed in ivy sits atop
the cupboard. Nearby, a 19th-century English
bamboo fireplace screen repeats the romantic mood.*

*Gail enjoys female artists, and their paintings fill the
wall above the antique English writing desk left, where
family photos mix with a bronze bust of a woman.*

Above a niche sparkling with majolica, left, whimsical trompe l'oeil
ivy ornaments a wall. An ivy topiary below it serves to befuddle the senses.
Where does nature stop and art begin?

Color and pattern frolic merrily throughout the living room above. Gail
chose pink—a favorite color—for the mantel. To ensure maximum
sunlight, a valance decorated with fringe replaces curtains. Gail calls it
"the window's eyebrows and eyelashes." An ornately painted chest of
drawers trimmed in black marble stands behind the sofa.

The bedroom right *is the most romantic room. A cherub watches over the Ghents as they sleep beneath headboards decorated with gilt and petit point roses.*

❧

The romantic aura that fills the house spills into the backyard below, *where a brick path winds to a stream through an expanse of grass.*

On a carefree Christmas holiday in England, an epiphany, of sorts, took place. Gail fell in love with Victorian and Edwardian luxury and the zest for excess of both eras.

Soon after that, the Ghents sent their younger child off to college, Gail closed her shop, and they looked forward to a period of rest and reflection. Instead, through a bit of serendipity, the Ghents happened upon a house. "As much as I loved our old home," says Gail, "I always knew there was another house in our future, something more comfortable. The old house had gorgeous, huge trees, but I could never grow a rose garden or herbs. There were things I hadn't done in my life, things that needed to be fulfilled."

*T*he newly discovered house seemed worldly wise beyond its mere 65 years. It had been empty for six months, but Gail could see past the sad decay and neglect. "I dragged my poor husband over to see it and said, 'This is what I want. This is

my house.' He's such a good-hearted fellow," laughs Gail. "There was no debate, we just did it. We approached the whole thing tongue in cheek. That's how life is."

Built at the apex of a rolling hill, the house now has a front yard where Gail's English perennial garden brims with wisteria that twines its way up and over the colonnaded entry. Inside, the botanical theme also prevails: from the bamboo fire screen to the dining room wallpaper festooned with tulips and lilacs to the engaging majolica. Ivy—English, of course—beams from on high and cascades down fronts of cupboards or creeps delicately up the walls, over paintings, and onto the ceiling.

*I*f flora, in its multifaceted aspect, is the leitmotiv of the house, then little faces—be they classical cherubs or Staffordshire dogs—are a minor but cherished theme. Cherubs smile down from many an intimate spot, and dogs sit in eager anticipation on a bureau or peer from behind a vase. "They're welcoming and happy," says Gail. "I enjoy them!"

Gail also enjoys female artists. The portrait of a woman in pink above the mantel in the living room is by 19th-century French artist Suzanne Hurel. Just above a portrait of flowers by St. Louis artist Kathryn Cherry (*page 98, bottom left*) is the endearing painting of a puppy demolishing a hat. This is the single artistic effort of Edd's great-aunt Lucy, who painted the picture just to show she could do as well as other family members.

Deeper and deeper Gail immerses herself into her paintings. The visions she gathers of languid days long past are artistically rendered in her home. Life, after all, is to be approached tongue in cheek. □

August

*THE KEY ELEMENTS
OF NEOTRADITIONAL STYLE—
SIMPLICITY AND ROMANCE—RESONATE
IN THIS CHICAGO HOME*

STATE
OF THE
Art

BY MIKE BUTLER

PHOTOGRAPHY BY JESSIE WALKER
PRODUCED WITH MARISA DIRKS AND SALLY MAUER
INTERIOR DESIGN BY LON HABKIRK

A diehard traditionalist somewhere walks into her living room and pauses. Her eyes dart from one piece of 18th-century wood furniture to another. It's not her anymore. It's too fussy, too serious. Somewhere else, a strict modernist sits in a 20th-century sling armchair and surveys his leather-and-chrome domain. It's not working for him. It's all too cold, too slick. Somewhere else still, a couple wonders what to do with a jumble of inherited antiques and joint purchases.

Over these troubled waters, neotraditional style builds a bridge. Homeowners who walk this span between a rich past and an uncertain future rediscover romance, simplicity, and comfort. More important, they find the courage to express their own personal style.

Offering furniture for the first time only 18 months ago, The Crate and Barrel in Chicago has become a leading outfitter of neotraditional style. Furnished and designed by the firm's creative director, Lon Habkirk, the North Shore home featured on these pages captures the magic that can happen after the furniture leaves the showroom floor.

In the neotraditional living room right, *furnishings of diverse heritages blend harmoniously into an eclectic but cohesive whole. The chair is made in Italy for The Crate and Barrel, of Chicago, and the sofas are adapted from originals found in an English country house. The Scandinavian painted armoire, an example of the antiques the Chicago furniture store also sells, contributes to the international theme.*

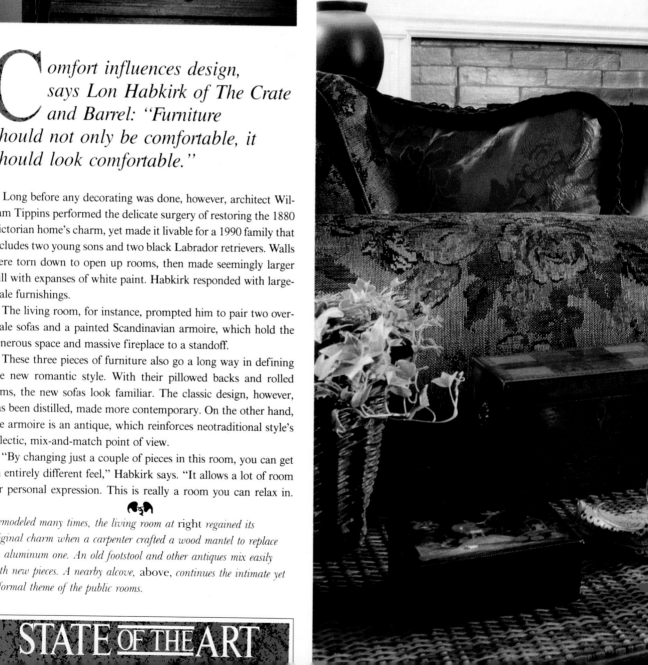

*C*omfort influences design, says Lon Habkirk of The Crate and Barrel: "Furniture should not only be comfortable, it should look comfortable."

Long before any decorating was done, however, architect William Tippins performed the delicate surgery of restoring the 1880 Victorian home's charm, yet made it livable for a 1990 family that includes two young sons and two black Labrador retrievers. Walls were torn down to open up rooms, then made seemingly larger still with expanses of white paint. Habkirk responded with large-scale furnishings.

The living room, for instance, prompted him to pair two over-scale sofas and a painted Scandinavian armoire, which hold the generous space and massive fireplace to a standoff.

These three pieces of furniture also go a long way in defining the new romantic style. With their pillowed backs and rolled arms, the new sofas look familiar. The classic design, however, has been distilled, made more contemporary. On the other hand, the armoire is an antique, which reinforces neotraditional style's eclectic, mix-and-match point of view.

"By changing just a couple of pieces in this room, you can get an entirely different feel," Habkirk says. "It allows a lot of room for personal expression. This is really a room you can relax in.

Remodeled many times, the living room at right *regained its original charm when a carpenter crafted a wood mantel to replace an aluminum one. An old footstool and other antiques mix easily with new pieces. A nearby alcove,* above, *continues the intimate yet informal theme of the public rooms.*

STATE OF THE ART

Directly over the living room, the master bedroom *above* owes its soothing atmosphere to a subtle interplay of neutrals. The tiger-maple four-poster and chests, although new, give the space a sense of history.

It has a traditional air to it without being intimidating or fussy." The designer carried the same theme into the adjacent dining room, where a hefty pine table balances the weight of another traditional fireplace.

In the master bedroom, directly over the living room, Habkirk seized an opportunity to get a little more sophisticated. The hand-crafted furniture provides further insight into The Crate and Barrel way of doing things. "We love to be able to support the artisans and craftsmen who are making these things. They really

❧

The homeowner's antique lace and a white duvet provide a perfect backdrop for the needlepoint pillows on the bed opposite. *The same principle applies to the white canvas-covered wing chair in the second-floor landing area* above. *No doubt once covered with a dark stain, the 110-year-old staircase in the entry hall* right *now makes a stunning first impression in white.*

STATE OF THE ART

Chefs-
d'œuvre

The neotraditional movement is not a passing fancy to retailers like The Crate and Barrel. "It's definitely our direction for the '90s," says creative director Lon Habkirk.

are the heirlooms of the future," says Habkirk. A husband-and-wife-owned company in the Berkshires in Massachusetts makes the Shaker-inspired four-poster and chests. The tiger-maple pieces are signed and dated. Similarly, a Massachusetts blacksmith forged the iron table from The Crate and Barrel's design.

Neotraditional wouldn't live up to its name if it didn't allow for surprises, and Habkirk took advantage of the style's relaxed rules. On the second-floor stair landing, for example, a natty white canvas covers the time-honored form of a wing chair. "Sometimes, with traditional forms like that, you really miss the beauty if they're done in a predictable damask fabric," Habkirk says.

Instead of expected white, a bleached finish on the wicker furniture in the screened porch prompts a double take, all the better to appreciate the romantic lines and intricate weaving. And when is the last time you saw a hunter-green sisal rug and a table lamp used on a sun porch?

"This whole look is playful and a lot of fun for people," says Habkirk. "It takes the very best of our history and brings it into the present and uses it in a fresh, new way. It's not a formula. The very staid, traditional style of decorating was a formula. The very strict modern style was a formula. This breaks out of all that and sets everyone free to be creative and self-expressive." □

Country Queen Anne-style chairs pull up to an oval pine table in the informal dining room opposite. *The chairs look almost contemporary in their purified forms and black-painted finishes. The screened porch* above *functions like a summer living room for the homeowners. A sisal rug provides its share of greenery.*

STATE OF THE ART

A Federal-style New England farmhouse expresses the refined sensibilities of its cosmopolitan owners.

FEDERAL EXPRESSION

BY DAN WEEKS

PHOTOGRAPHS BY D. RANDOLPH FOULDS
PRODUCED BY ESTELLE BOND GURALNICK

❝ *The entry hall* **opposite** *sets the theme for the rest of the house: Most furniture is Early American yet the architecture and finishes are rich in Federal-style detail.*

❝ *The charming simplicity of this Federal home* **bottom right** *with its brick walks and terraced herb gardens is readily apparent from the street.*

❝ *The arched breezeway, stone well, and brick path,* **top right,** *tie the house and barn together.*

❝ *Created by enlarging and enclosing a sun porch, the parlor* **left** *offers a wonderful view of both the park and the gardens. It also features spectacular architectural embellishment. The homeowners brought all the furniture with them, including the old Oriental rug and the 18th-century Queen Anne tea table. The chairs and sofa were recovered especially for this room.*

❝ *A close collaboration between homeowner, decorators, carpenter, and artist produced the fluted columns* **above** *and other details that embellish this room. Even the baseboards are marbleized.*

The rich and colorful interior of this picture-postcard New England farmhouse shows what sophisticated taste can express when freed from rigid convention—in this case, by the skillful mixing of Georgian and Federal styles. The house combines a stunning collection of Early American and Queen Anne furniture with the broad color palette and rich wallpapers and fabrics that characterize the Federal period.

Located a short stroll from the center of a quiet New England mill town, the home was built in the late 1700s. Some years ago, the owners purchased the house for their son, who was in business nearby.

Business later took their son elsewhere, but not before the couple developed an affection for the house, its surrounding gardens, and the 200-acre park and nature preserve that abuts the property. When they decided they were ready for the convenience of a smaller home in a country town, they sold their big, remote colonial and moved into the farmhouse, lock, stock, and 300-year-old furniture.

All of their previous homes featured 18th-century interiors: paneling painted in antique colors and white plaster walls.

N O SPARTAN COLONIAL, THIS 200-YEAR-OLD HOUSE COMBINES 18TH-CENTURY FURNITURE WITH RICH ARCHITECTURAL AND DECORATIVE DETAILING.

But this house was different. It had undergone some changes over the years—its first remodeling was in 1830—so the new owners didn't feel obliged to be purists. Freed from the constraints of an 18th-century interior for the first time, the couple combined their furnishings with Federal-style architectural detailing, fabrics, and painted and papered backdrops.

The result is a house that expresses the best of two centuries of taste. Key to the success of the melding of styles was selecting elements of each that would reinforce one another, then using color and pattern to further tie the elements together.

The hardest choice to make was the first: deciding which paper to use for

Early 18th-century Queen Anne chairs and drop-leaf tables, right, grace the dining room. The silvery gray, bittersweet, and navy blue backdrop complements the hues of a Heriz Oriental rug.

The dining room's circa-1750 pewter cabinet above is filled with pieces collected over a lifetime.

116

A brick terrace with raised beds set off by stone, **left**, was added by the homeowners as a transitional space between the house and the lower garden. The couple also designed the fence on the far side of the terrace to match the existing arches of the breezeway. The cream-colored paint **below** *delineates the new parlor, which was formerly an open porch. From the brick terrace, you can follow stone steps to the lower flower garden, then through the gate* **above** *to the back of the property, which is planted with flowers, vegetables, and herbs.*

the front hall. Designers Rudy Hendrics and George Sattler fueled the owners' rapidly growing enthusiasm for their new house with a carefully chosen preselection of appropriate treatments and finishes. The designers and their clients made the final selection together, after spending many hours crouched on the floor of the empty house, poring over samples. The time was well invested: The color scheme for the entire home flowed from the foyer's wallpaper.

Since the house was quite plain inside when they acquired it, the couple worked closely with Hendrics, Sattler, and a highly skilled carpenter to add detail. Although it looks original, much of the interior architectural embellishment— paneling, custom molding, shelves, beams, cornices, and trim around windows and doors—was added recently.

Hendrics and Sattler are experts in period houses, and they suggested many of the improvements. Other improvements— such as the reproduction 18th-century corner cupboard in the dining room— were the homeowners' ideas.

The couple spotted an antique cupboard in the dining room of a local tavern. They liked the piece so much that they took their carpenter to lunch there to see it. After dessert, he took measurements of the piece and created a duplicate, which he installed in the couple's dining room.

The cupboard is painted a bright orange in contrast to the room's silvery gray background; and the piece now houses a collection of antique china.

❝ *The walls of the spare room* **right** *are covered in the same fabric as the bed skirt and quilted coverlet, and a paisley print on the same ground makes an effective bed canopy.*
Both the ball-foot blanket chest at the foot of the bed and the antique dresser feature their original finishes.

❝ *A primitive portrait on wood and an old blanket chest in its original finish,* **above,** *are part of the 18th-century charm of the spare room.*

❝ *Shades of mustard and old red warm the master bedroom* **left.** *A collection of Shaker boxes tops the early, raised-panel cupboard.*

ATTERN AND COLOR—BOLD YET WELL
THOUGHT-OUT BY THE HOMEOWNERS—GIVE THIS
HOUSE ITS PUNCH AND VIVACITY.

The library, with its book-lined walls, handsome beams, and warm colors, was formerly the living room. All architectural detail was added, and the new woodwork painted a "cooked shrimp" color against off-white walls.

The house's tour de force is the parlor (see *pages 54* and *55*). Created by extending and enclosing an existing sun porch, it was designed from scratch as an 18th-century room. It is hard to decide the room's most striking feature: the color scheme or the decorative painting.

Glazed and painted woodwork and beams in a custom mix of brownish purple are balanced by off-white walls. The same colors can be seen in the French toile window treatments. The decorative painting mixes several 18th-century techniques—marbleizing, feathering, herringboning, and faux graining—to stunning effect. Overlooking the house's gardens, the room is a favorite spot for reading, conversation, and fireside relaxing.

Perhaps the most significant aspect of the parlor—and the entire home—is that none of the attention paid to the home's architecture and backdrops has detracted from the beauty of the couple's impressive collection of colonial furniture. The homeowners credit the success of their blend of styles to careful attention to color and pattern—and to their evolving confidence in expanding their own purist sensibilities.

They broke a few of their own rules with this house, they confess. They also confess to having had fun doing it, and being very pleased with the results. □

❝ *Called the recipe room because its shelves are filled with cookbooks, the upstairs sitting room* **right** *features a tree-and-bird hand-printed wallpaper. Dormer eaves are accentuated with rope-paper borders.*

❝ *The library* **above** *pairs an early gateleg table with very old banister-back side chairs. The chandelier and tavern table are also 18th century. Custom dhurrie rugs use colors taken from the room's fabrics.*

❝ *Custom cabinets in the remodeled kitchen* **left** *harmonize with the tile floor. French copper pots are poised to prepare a gourmet meal.*

HE HOMEOWNERS CONFESS TO HAVING BROKEN A
FEW RULES WITH THIS HOUSE. THEY HAD FUN DOING
IT AND ARE VERY PLEASED WITH THE RESULTS.

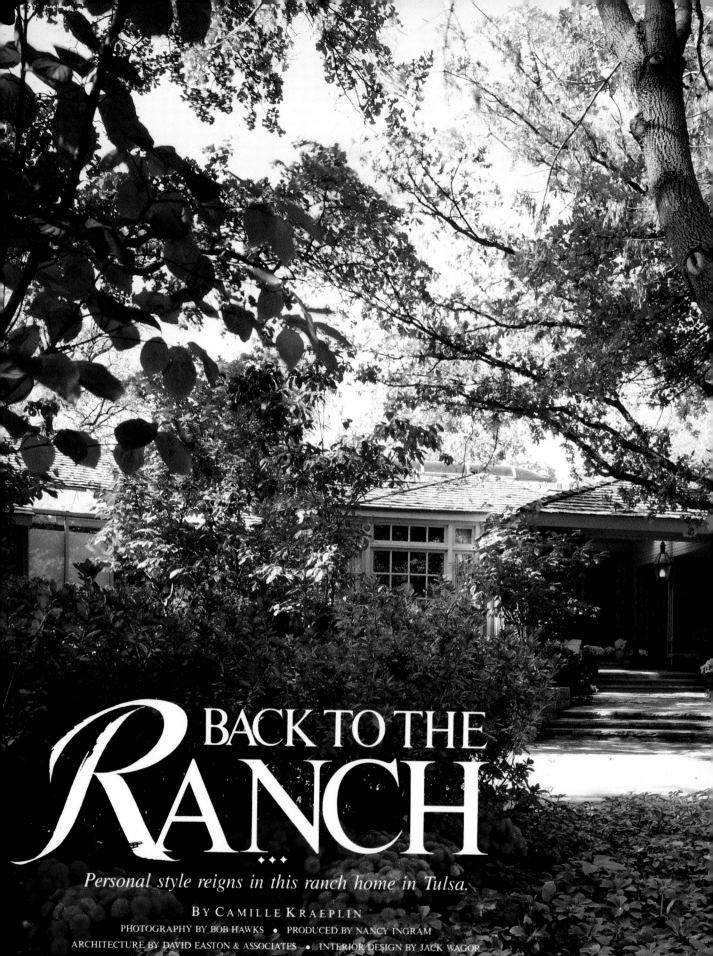

BACK TO THE
RANCH

Personal style reigns in this ranch home in Tulsa.

BY CAMILLE KRAEPLIN

PHOTOGRAPHY BY BOB HAWKS • PRODUCED BY NANCY INGRAM

ARCHITECTURE BY DAVID EASTON & ASSOCIATES • INTERIOR DESIGN BY JACK WAGOR

K ing and Lee Kirchner's ranch-
style house sits atop rolling,
wooded acreage in Tulsa. A spacious, sunny home, it is the perfect setting for the
Kirchners' unique mix of European antiques and contemporary American western art. Personal style abounds in this
updated "home on the range."

When the Kirchners first saw this property, they fell in love with the lush grounds
planted with mature elms, oaks, and ma-
ples. They were less enamored with the
dark, low-ceilinged rooms and dated fix-
tures that prevailed in the rambling 1950s-
era stone-and-cedar house.

They called on the New York architectural firm of David Easton and Associates
to update the structure and expand the
existing space. Ceilings were raised, windows were replaced by expansive window
walls, and an entire new wing was added

Oklahoma natives King and Lee Kirchner,
above, *share a love of wide-open spaces*
typical of the American Southwest and a
connoisseur's interest in collectibles from
Europe and the Far East. The Kirchners'
remodeled ranch-style home left *is*
approached via a driveway that meanders
over a bridge and circles a lake to the front
courtyard. The sophisticated redesign makes
the most of the home's country setting by
integrating indoor and outdoor living areas.

125

In King's library, left, the walls have been glazed to resemble red leather
books. *Though the room reflects King's personality, it features early 19th-century hand-colored
lithographs of bobcats and wildcats selected by Lee. The entryway of the house,* below, *is
testimony to both of the Kirchners' strong personal tastes, balancing bold western
art by Paul Pletka with French antiques such as the twin oak benches upholstered in
black-and-white cowhide and the antique toy wooden horse in the foreground.*

to the original structure. Of the sizable
project, Lee says, "We felt like we were
remodeling an old house and building a
new one at the same time."

When it came to the home's interiors,
Lee, an artist with a penchant for bright
color, had definite ideas. She found in interior designer Jack Wagor, of Dallas, a
shared viewpoint. "I've always admired
Jack's work," says Lee. "It's timeless. And
I particularly like his color sense."

A harmonious, albeit intense, collaboration of homeowners, architect, and interior designer resulted in a home alive with
light, color, and beauty.

The home's architectural and interior
scheme unfolds from a spacious, light-
filled front hall. "The entry is the back-
bone of the house," says Lee. "All the

rooms fan out from here, and it sets the
tone for the rest of the rooms."

The entry is softly illuminated by a
curved, vaulted skylight and punctuated
by boldly colored, large paintings of Cus-
ter and Crazy Horse. With such an intro-
duction, the rooms beyond promise
wonderful surprises and treasures.

They don't disappoint. Every space
telegraphs the Kirchners' interests, tal-
ents, and personal tastes.

King's family background shows up in
small touches—his childhood cowboy
boots sit atop the mantel in the study—
and also in more prominent ways.

Raised on a ranch in western Oklahoma
and named for his grandfather, King has
fond memories of a childhood ranch-style
home. "Granddad made a bit of money in

*W*ith its soaring cathedral ceiling,
the living room is a dramatic setting for the
Kirchners' diverse collection of
furnishings and art. A vivid oil painting by
Fritz Scholder draws the eye to the
classic 18th-century French stone fireplace
mantel. Flanking the fireplace are
17th-century Spanish candle holders and
lamps fashioned from Chinese wood
figures. A cream custom-woven carpet and
oversize sofas upholstered in a lush fabric
add warmth and texture to the room.
Oklahoma City artist Suzanne Mears
crafted the ceramic plate top. The plate
takes its place alongside 19th-century
Japanese bronze candle holders and antique
mother-of-pearl and tortoise on the
reproduction coffee table by Minton Spidell.
An array of found objects displayed on a
country French sofa table, above, reflects
Lee Kirchner's disparate tastes.

129

Southwestern touches abound in the Kirchners' study left *and* below
*from an original oil painting by Paul Pletka to the small timber beams that frame
the ceiling to the pint-size cowboy boots that King wore as a boy on a ranch in western
Oklahoma. On one side of the bookcase is a collection of antique Mexican masks;
on the other, a TV is discreetly hidden behind painted panoic. Lee, pictured*
below, *had the walls glazed in a light terra-cotta to resemble adobe.*

the oil business in his day too," says King, a prominent oilman himself. "Granddad built a house in Santa Fe, and I spent every summer as a child in that sprawling, sun-filled house. I loved it."

It isn't surprising that almost every room in King's home has floor-to-ceiling windows that welcome the brilliant Oklahoma sun.

Lee's presence also is felt in every room—in the warm palette of textures and in the intriguing accessories that personalize each space. Wagor explains that while traveling, Lee is always on the lookout for treasures for her home. The designer advised: "Buy what you like. You can tie it all together with color."

The success of that strategy is proven in the master suite, where a terra-cotta and cream color scheme provides a quiet canvas for disparate found objects, such as the *santos* (artistic religious renderings, especially of saints) from South America and the Venetian mirror over the fireplace. Lee retreats to the room after a day's work at the easel. "It's a wonderful place to be, with the view of the lake and the little orchard outside," she comments.

Wagor says the Kirchners' house is eclectic in the truest sense. Each room exemplifies personal vision. The living room shown on *pages 128* and *129,* for instance, is a melting pot of diverse elements—each with individual strengths.

The room's focal-point fireplace is surrounded by an 18th-century French stone mantel. Above it, a contemporary painting by American Fritz Scholder is flanked

In the kitchen right, *the oversize marble-topped island dominates. Comfortable barstools pull up to the island to accommodate diners or extra cooks. The 18th-century French farm table in the dining room* below *is set for an informal wine and cheese tasting, typical of the Kirchners' relaxed style of entertaining. An antique Scandinavian goat carving,* bottom, *stands atop an 18th-century Louis XV chest. Above the chest is an antique plate rack, which displays a collection of contemporary pottery and other artifacts.*

by 17th-century Spanish candle holders. Stately lamps on each side of the fireplace are made of 18th-century Chinese figures.

This unusual composition and others in the room are underscored by a calm, monochromatic color scheme. Neutral walls, carpet, and upholstery fabrics, enlivened by touches of red, allow accessories to shine while providing a harmonious background.

Nubby textures prevent neutrals from becoming flat and lend a casualness to the room. Plump, overscaled chairs and large ottomans add physical comfort—a characteristic King insisted upon throughout.

The Kirchners' appreciation of nature's beauty also provides restful continuity throughout the house. Every room is planned to bring the outdoors in. In the dining room, a floor-to-ceiling bay window affords diners seated at the 18th-century French farm table an intimate view of the groomed courtyard. A French door off the room opens to a path that leads to an arbor-covered swimming pool.

Even in the master bath and dressing

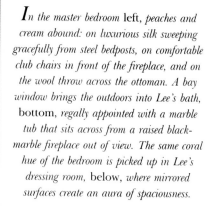

In the master bedroom left, *peaches and cream abound: on luxurious silk sweeping gracefully from steel bedposts, on comfortable club chairs in front of the fireplace, and on the wool throw across the ottoman. A bay window brings the outdoors into Lee's bath,* bottom, *regally appointed with a marble tub that sits across from a raised black-marble fireplace out of view. The same coral hue of the bedroom is picked up in Lee's dressing room,* below, *where mirrored surfaces create an aura of spaciousness.*

areas the Kirchners have expanses of glass and custom windows that drink up the outdoors. In King's shower a brass ship's porthole is inset into the wall. On temperate days, it is opened so fresh air can be enjoyed in the shower.

A bay window looking out on woods is the backdrop to Lee's luxurious marble whirlpool tub. But privacy is thought of, too. At the flick of a switch, electronically controlled mirrored doors slide across the window for complete seclusion.

The Kirchners and Wagor admit that the intense togetherness of the renovation, when the designer all but moved in, was trying at times. "We were like a fighting, feuding family. But in the end, everyone got what they wanted," says Wagor. "This house is the culmination of a good architect, good craftsmen, King's expertise, and Lee's great style." At which point, Lee quickly intercedes, "Jack is too modest. He's a genius." □

October

New England
SPIRIT

A
Singular
Serenity

BY ESTELLE BOND GURALNICK

PHOTOGRAPHY BY D. RANDOLPH FOULDS

Calm interiors spiced by
accents from many cultures
reflect the refined sense of color
Betty Fleischman has brought
to her October Mountain Farm
in Massachusetts.

Chastely elegant yet warm and inviting, the living room above juxtaposes old chairs and a sofa—freshened by white linen—with some unusual antiques. An old French toy horse stands atop a long American harvest table. The dramatically rendered Early American Windsor chair faces a diversity of baskets. The workings of the mid-19th-century French Morbier clock were bought in New Jersey 22 years before Betty found the Mobier case in upstate New York.

Though October Mountain Farm was already named, its identifying sign, left, was designed by Betty. Plantings around the lamppost bloom from spring's daffodils to fall's purple monkshood and yellow coreopsis. Opposite, daughters Daria, left, and Deborah take tea in the living room. "They've been antiquing with me since childhood," says Betty, "so this is very much their house, too."

lizabeth Brady Fleischman, known as Betty to family and friends, remembers her first impression of October Mountain Farm as though it were yesterday—instead of 10 years ago. Not only was there a beautiful old farmhouse with outbuildings on a pastoral 5-acre property, but the land backed onto October Mountain, which is part of the Berkshires, a mountain chain in western Massachusetts. "It felt like a private world," she says. "There was a sense of leaving everything else behind."

Before moving to the rural region, Betty and her husband, Sidney, had lived in New Jersey, Manhattan, and the Virgin Islands. It was during those years that they brought up two daughters, Deborah and Daria, while Betty pursued her lifelong passion for collecting. "Wherever I am, I'm always on the trail of something," she says with relish. "I head out looking for the undiscovered waiting for me."

While the girls were still little, Betty combined parenting with studying for a degree in interior design from the New York School of Interior Design. Credentials in order, she continued with courses at Parsons School of Design, also in New York City, and then started to take on private decorating commissions. For a five-year period, she and some partners ran an art and antiques gallery.

Initially, the move to a country town like Lenox, Massachusetts, was fueled by a desire for a part-time retreat from New York City. "The cultural variety of Lenox was a big attraction, particularly the music at the annual Tanglewood Music Festival," Betty says. "We wanted a taste of the peaceful life but not in an area where the only diversion was to go out to dinner." In addition, she was ready to put aside professional decorating in favor of opening her own antiques shop.

Either her request to the real-estate agent for an old house with outbuildings was right on target or Lady Luck was in the mood to beam. In either case, October Mountain Farm was the first and only property the Fleischmans saw. "I went back a second time with my

A Virgin Islands discovery, the 19th-century, Pennsylvania tiger-maple highboy in the living room below is handsomely topped by Japanese lacquerware and a beautiful 18th-century Chinese porcelain bird.

The small sitting room left is a favorite Fleischman family spot for reading and television. "It's also nice to have morning coffee here, because it's so sunny," says Betty. Chairs from a tag sale and an old love seat are unified by cotton slipcovers striped in pale yellow and white. The new needlepoint rug takes its colors from Betty's collection of majolica started long ago. The furniture arrangement shows her penchant for angled seating, teamed with ottomans for comfort. Lamps, once old English candlesticks, have silk shades. A small table by the bookshelves is one Betty carried on a plane from Ireland. Rose medallion china fills the rear cupboards.

141

Serenely restful, the master bedroom right
displays a rare pair of white wedding quilts from
1876 on the old spool beds, topped by Italian
flowered wool throws. A French art nouveau bronze
lamp sits atop the night table. The ceramic Minton
garden stand was Daria's as a child.
American cottage furniture from the 1800s looks
right in the small guest room above.
Pink chintz at the windows and a pretty turn-of-the-
century quilt are country touches.

daughter Deb to see if the pull was as
strong, and it was," recalls Betty. "The
house actually called to me."

To some, the appeal of the early 19th-
century homestead might not have been
as readily apparent. Wood paneling was
down-home knotty pine, and there were
wall coverings in every room—even on
some ceilings. "There was nothing bad
about it," Betty says, "it just was not for
me. The previous owner really loved the
house, had kept it in good repair, and
hadn't disturbed the architecture. I saw
through the distractions, and knew I
could perform a transformation with
paint and attention to small details."

Those small details included five
buckets of hinges and hardware from
French doors and windows that went
out to be vatted and cleaned. Presto!
From under a dozen coats of paint,
gleaming brass emerged. Walls and
woodwork were painted pale creamy

In the dining room above, American thumb-back Windsor chairs pull up to an antique country French table. Old storage boxes make a pyramid on an early painted trunk made by the Hitchcock Co. Behind the table, two early still-life paintings hang above a cluster of Nantucket baskets on an American pine chest. The cubbyholes, seen close up at left, were probably meant to display teacups, but that's not Betty's style. Instead, she brought home children's blocks from an auction for a touch of whimsy.

Betty likes the open space opposite between the dining room and the kitchen. For informal entertaining, the pass-through becomes a buffet server. On the windowsill, toy animals from an old ark—a Christmas present from her daughters—march along behind a small English bar. The lamp is Chinese porcelain. Seating includes a Shaker rush-seat rocker, an English Windsor armchair, and an Early American high chair.

beige and highlighted with white moldings. All the original old pine floors were buffed and burnished. In the kitchen, old red linoleum gave way to a new hardwood floor later painted by local artists Richard and Brenda Birtel to resemble one in a 17th-century French château. "They caught it perfectly," Betty says.

Betty's mastery of understated design achieves an elegant sense of timeless simplicity by mixing elements from different cultures. American antiques consort easily with French and English pieces, all sparked by collections of the Orient. "I try to buy the best I can afford," she says. "In fact, that's a good rule for everyone."

Another reflection of Betty's understated style is a preference for monotones for her background. "When you have good architecture, beautiful windows and moldings, and nice antiques, they shouldn't have to compete with color," she says. The neutrality of her sisal flooring pleases her: "I like its simplicity. It makes all woods look even better."

She has other strong predilections, too. She calls herself "a nut for painted floors, which are a great idea from the past." She likes ottomans for comfort, and sofas placed on the diagonal. She also enjoys entertaining, and believes houses can and should change along with the owners' personal interests.

"I think a house should be fun rather than serious, in flux rather than static," Betty says. "For me, it's second nature to shift things around from time to time, sometimes just for the whimsy of putting things in unexpected places." Her French pull-toy horse, for instance, resides in the living room but is often on the move, sometimes lording over the dining room table.

Daughters Deborah Deck and Daria Sherman think Betty's eclectic style is part of her essence. "Mother is unique," Deborah says. "She's very talented but low-key. One of her strengths is the remarkable way she visualizes. She can walk into a room and tell us just what should go where, and, you know, she's always right!"

Illustrating Betty's distinctive

approach, Daria says: "Mother drives a 1956 Bentley that was her fortieth-birthday present. At toll booths, she uses an antique collection basket to hand the money out because the car has right-hand drive. She has flair! We're lucky to have her."

New England has long since exerted its own pull on the Fleischmans. At first, Sidney juggled his work schedule in the textile business, and they kept a small apartment in New York. Three years ago he retired, and now October Mountain Farm is their full-time home. On weekends, the house is apt to hum with visits from family and houseguests.

"We all go through different periods in life," Betty observes, "but I'm constantly learning with each new experience." Betty couldn't have chosen a more idyllic setting for the process. □

New England
SPIRIT

Old-world style and New World spirit pair off in the suburban Boston home of Jill Katz and John Madfis.

Doing the
CONTINENTAL

BY MIKE BUTLER

PHOTOGRAPHY BY D. RANDOLPH FOULDS
INTERIOR DESIGN BY BETSY SPEERT
PRODUCED BY ESTELLE BOND GURALNICK

Not a stick of furniture graced the inside of the house on the big day 10 years ago, but that didn't matter. The wedding of Jill Katz and John Madfis was taking place in the backyard, where the azaleas, rhododendrons, and peonies were in full bloom and scenting a perfect spring day.

When the moving trucks did pull up later to the old Dutch colonial west of Boston, however, the marriage of furnishings was less than perfect. Jill owned a lot of art deco furniture that had belonged to her grandmother. John had outfitted his apartment with beach house rattan.

On their trips to shop for furniture together, Jill says, "We basically bought rooms right off the

A MARKETING CONSULTANT FOR CBS AND OTHER CLIENTS, JILL KATZ MADFIS, PICTURED ON PAGE 149, WORKS OUT OF AN OFFICE ON THE THIRD FLOOR OF HER BOSTON HOME, *ABOVE.* A PAINTED FLOOR IN THE ENTRYWAY *LEFT* GIVES A HINT OF COLORS AND PATTERNS TO COME.

PAPERED WALLS IN THE LIVING ROOM GIVE THE APPEARANCE OF RAG PAINTING AND PROVIDE A UNIFYING BACKGROUND FOR THE ROOM'S PROFUSION OF BOLD COLORS AND PATTERNS.

showroom floor. We tended to go for very trendy, hot looks. We were loud and kind of mixed up."

Years rolled by. Jill and John juggled the demands of two kids, Jake and Molly, and two careers. The way they used their living spaces became as jumbled as their furnishings.

They watched television and spent most of their time in a small den, which was formerly the dining room. The original living room had turned into a dining area but served as little more than a passageway between the den and sun-room.

Several years ago, John, a leasing agent for shopping malls, hired interior designer Betsy Speert to redecorate his office. She examined John and Jill's predicament on the home front and convinced the Madfises that they needed to use their house more efficiently.

By sealing off one of the two doors to the sun-room, the living room stopped being a tunnel and gained more wall space. The sun-room also gained enough wall space to function as a family room with the requisite electronic equipment. The den became a dining room once again.

*J*ill *conveyed the mood she wanted for her rooms to interior designer Betsy Speert in an unusual way: "I had a Ralph Lauren needlepoint handbag that I really love. I showed it to Betsy and said, 'That's the look I want for the house.' She got it, and it worked."*

ACCESSORIES ARE FOR THE BIRDS IN THE DINING ROOM *OPPOSITE* AND *BELOW*. UNFINISHED REGENCY-STYLE CHAIRS WERE CUSTOM-PAINTED TO COORDINATE WITH THE PAPERED, MOSS-GREEN WALLS. THE ROOM HAS A SENSE OF HISTORY, THANKS TO THE HANDSOME REPRODUCTION TABLE, SIDEBOARD, AND OIL PAINTINGS.

Two people coming together with their stuff. That's the way all relationships start. We were very loud and kind of mixed up.

— JILL KATZ MADFIS

Jill and John had figured it would take a family room addition to solve their space problems. With that solved by minor remodeling of the sun-room, they diverted their resources to giving the kitchen a face-lift and creating a focused decorating style in the living and dining rooms and master bedroom. "We got rid of some of the wrong stuff we had, so it was like starting over," Jill says.

To convey the kind of look she wanted, Jill held up a favorite Ralph Lauren needlepoint handbag, and Speert took it from there. The old-world traditional scheme that emerged, however, also kept

THE MASTER BEDROOM *RIGHT* AND *ABOVE*
OWES ITS ENGLISH COUNTRY AMBIENCE TO A
MIX OF ANTIQUES AND NEW PIECES.
JUST-FOR-FUN TASSELS ON THE BEDPOSTS REPEAT
THE HOME'S COLOR SCHEME.

*I*n the long run, we added up our expenses and figured out that what we'd done was more economical than putting on an addition.

—— JILL KATZ MADFIS

the kids in mind along with John's modernist love for strong colors, patterns, and textures. "It wasn't my project," Jill says. "It was our project. I kept saying to Betsy that we needed comfort, rooms that kids can come into and not destroy."

In the entry, a painted floor executed by decorative painter Alan Carroll employs traditional octagons interspersed with small squares, but the unusual rose color gives a hint of surprises to come. "It's safer to do cream and black," Speert says, "but using color is truer to John's tastes."

An old Oriental rug inspired the from-the-ground-up scheme in the living room. The seating pieces are new, but their overstuffed forms, trimmed with braiding and welting, create an impression that the room evolved over generations. "We read there, talk on the phone, and the kids use the ottoman in front of the sofa as a stage for puppet shows," Jill says. "It's wonderful. We use every room."

Although they were surprised at first that they could share an appreciation for traditional design, John and Jill didn't settle on it as a compromise. They took that road because it offered them a chance to express their creativity and truly make the home their own. "We're so yuppie, so typical of everyone in our group, that in a way we were rebelling," Jill says. "We wanted our home to look as though it hadn't just happened, but instead as though we'd always had it." □

GERMAN CABINETRY IN THE KITCHEN
RIGHT CREATES THE FEEL OF A PATISSERIE.
SPEERT DESIGNED THE PATTERN
FOR THE STOCK MOSAIC TILES AS WELL AS THE
PAINTED CHAIRS AND TABLE BASE.

154

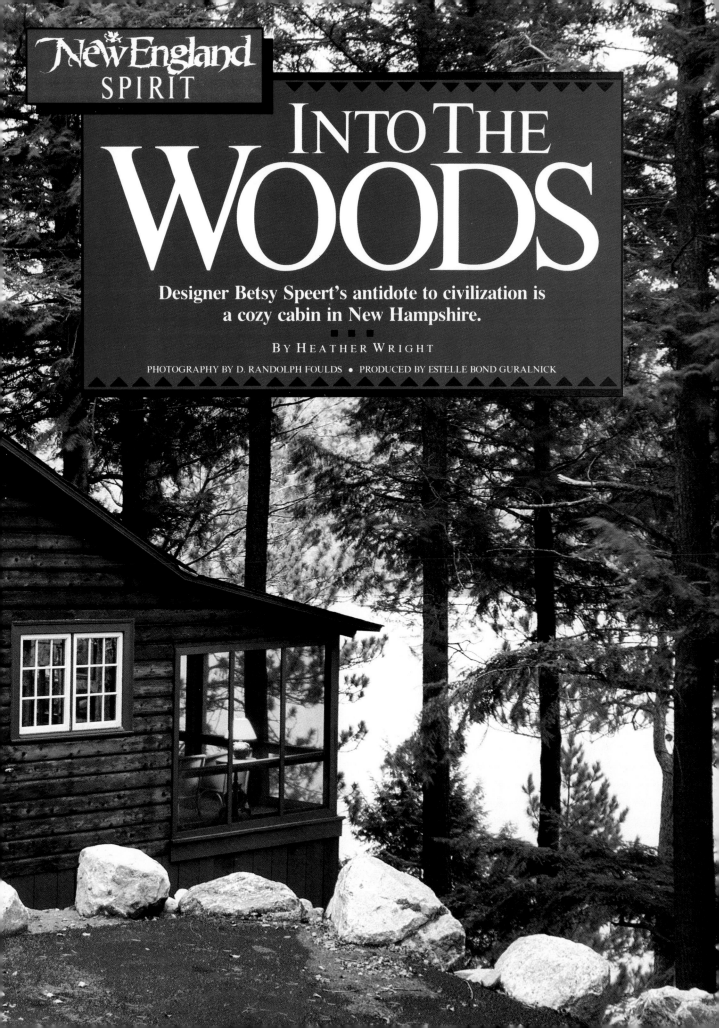

INTO THE WOODS

Designer Betsy Speert's antidote to civilization is
a cozy cabin in New Hampshire.

■ ■ ■

BY HEATHER WRIGHT

PHOTOGRAPHY BY D. RANDOLPH FOULDS ● PRODUCED BY ESTELLE BOND GURALNICK

It's late summer on Sunapee Lake in southern New Hampshire. The sun has set; a warm breeze rustles in the trees; tiny waves lap at the shore. Betsy Speert is curled up on the screened-in porch of her cedar log cabin nestled in the woods. A loon's cry echoes across shimmering waters.

"The magic here lies in the sense of escape," says Betsy of the place she calls home almost every weekend from April to November. "This isn't just another house. It's *special.*"

Betsy's cabin is indeed special. Though less than two hours from Boston—where Betsy is a prominent interior designer with a schedule that is frenzied at best—it seems a million miles away from the chaos of city life. There are no horns blasting, no sirens wailing; no noisy neighbors, pretensions, or crowds. Just peace, tranquillity, and gracious wilderness.

It was August 1984 when Betsy first set eyes on her 60-year-old cabin. After seeing an

Betsy Speert, above, relaxes on the screened-in porch, which runs the length of the rear of the cabin. Says Betsy: "It's the best room in the house!"

The rustic table opposite is original to the cabin and is playfully set for Sunday brunch with carved Victorian Era bears. "When I return in spring, there always seem to be more of them!" Betsy says. Her frolicking bears can be found in every room in the house.

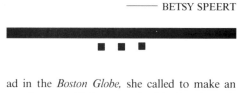

I DO LIKE MY CREATURE COMFORTS, BUT MY GOAL WAS TO CREATE THE FEELING OF A SPECIAL LITTLE CAMP.

—— BETSY SPEERT

■ ■ ■

ad in the *Boston Globe,* she called to make an appointment. "Bring your checkbook," the real-estate agent said. "*This* one won't last." Betsy had heard that line so many times she'd lost count; she shrugged it off. The moment she saw the cabin, though, she knew it was right. Her heart raced as she double-checked for her wallet and approached the front door.

A *fieldstone chimney is the natural focal point in the 13×19-foot living room. Its mantel is carved with a line from an old English poem by Edward FitzGerald: "Ah wilderness, were paradise enow." Betsy installed two large skylights (one seen at* **right**)*, to shed new light on the previously gloomy room. Between the far windows an old scorched bamboo étagère showcases more of Betsy's carved Victorian bears. Pillows made of vintage fabrics and kilim rugs complement the room's warm, textural ambience.*

Measuring just 600 square feet, Betsy's cabin is the equivalent of a tiny gem that has been cut simply and polished ever-so-slightly to bring out its natural brilliance. "One of the reasons I liked the cabin so much was that it needed so little improvement," Betsy says. "It was just waiting for my touch."

There were, of course, a few obvious problems. What troubled Betsy most was darkness. It was only after noon—when the sun was high enough to make its way in from above tall evergreens surrounding the cabin—that the gloom partially lifted. And the dark was intensified by the cabin's paneled walls and stone fireplace.

The galley kitchen at **right** is bright and lively. An old Welsh cupboard and a simple pine armoire frame a compact cooking area at the rear of the living room chimney. Betsy devised a pot rack of plumber's copper elbows and water pipe. The dining bump-out **above** has a 12-foot pitched roof.

▲ ▲ ▲ ▲ ▲ ▲

her an opportunity to explore new design expressions. While her interior design work in Boston is formal and opulent, here she can break rules, take chances, and have lots of fun doing it.

"Though I do like my creature comforts," she says, "my goal here was to create the feeling of a special little camp." As such, the cabin is chockfull of elements that heighten its rustic tenor. Pine armoires, rough-hewn tables, wicker, and bentwood chairs are prettily accented by old shawls, kilims, needlepoint, vintage fabric pillows, and a den full of Victorian bears. Each low-stress, high-style room blends personality, warmth, and humor.

Betsy is pleased with her accomplishments but has more plans in store. The room beneath the screened-in porch will someday be a sauna; the cabin garage would make a terrific year-round ski house. "There are lots of possibilities to contemplate," she says, smiling. For now, though, daylight is just about gone, and Betsy's first priority is some serious relaxation. □

■ ■ ■

I BELIEVE HOUSES
REALLY RESPOND TO
PEOPLE, AND
NOW I'M SURE THIS
HOUSE REALLY
LIKES ME.

—— BETSY SPEERT

Painting the wood white or pickling it was out of the question. It would disturb the warm rustic mood. Betsy's solution was skylights: two in the living room, two in the kitchen, and one in the loft above a section of the living room and master bedroom. Sun now streams in with new vigor but doesn't detract from the cabin's intrinsic charms.

A second problem Betsy needed to resolve was that her only dining space was in the living room. "It felt like a studio apartment," she says. To free the living room from double duty, a contractor designed a 5×9-foot eating-area addition to bump out from her tiny galley kitchen. The result was a vaulted glass niche with a panoramic view of the lake and mountains. Betsy completed the dramatic mood with a wonderful wood floor that is painted to mimic fieldstone, replete with trompe l'oeil cement grout.

This cabin is, above all, a well-deserved retreat. But Betsy does admit the place has given

The master bedroom above is a snug 9×9 feet. Cabbage-rose wallpaper, a cottage dresser, and an iron bed covered with a paisley shawl lend warmth.

Betsy's "grungy" bathroom, right, was transformed with new gypsum board and a white tile floor. The original bathtub was fitted with a bright chintz curtain.

December

A
Norwegian
CHRISTMAS
In
Illinois

BY KATHY KASTILAHN

PHOTOGRAPHY BY JESSIE WALKER

*Chicago architect Stephen Knutson
calls on his rich heritage
for holiday celebrating
with his family.*

Georgian revival design, a spacious layout, bright colors, and an abundance of exuberant Victorian furniture provide a rich backdrop for seasonal decorations in the living room of the Knutsons' Chicago apartment, right.

Stephen, Haakon, and Mary Knutson, below, *toast the season. The mantelpiece is typical of the apartment's fine detailing.*

"We ate seven times on Christmas Eve, and each time there was linen, silver, and flowers on the table," recalls Stephen Knutson, of the Christmas he spent with his Norwegian relatives many years ago.

"The tree was decorated with white lights and red-and-white paper Norwegian flags, and there were lots of candles burning," he continues. "After church, we opened presents, and the celebration went late into the night."

Every Christmas since, Stephen, along with his wife, Mary, and son, Haakon, have saluted family heritage by stringing rows and rows of Norwegian flags amid other ornaments, and welcoming friends and family to their gracious circa-1916 apartment on Chicago's North Shore.

Stephen's childhood Christmases were midwestern. "But after my Christmas

I love the heartiness and richness of Victorian pieces. They're big and fat and comfortable.

——— STEPHEN KNUTSON

Jul Nissen, *a Norwegian Christmas elf, perches on a present-laden table. Pieces of Norwegian rosemaling cover the walnut table by the fireplace, and a one-of-a-kind Gay Nineties parlor chair adds turn-of-the-century charm from its position upstage of the fire.*

*he tree trimming and hall decking take three days,
and we start the day after Thanksgiving. We each have . . .
lots of personal treasures. . . . After that I start baking.*

— MARY KNUTSON

in Norway," he continues, "my parents became more interested, too. Now on Christmas Eve my mother serves *bets,* a traditional food we've dubbed a Norwegian burrito. It's made with a flat bread called *lefse* that is rolled around boiled potatoes and fish."

Stephen's wife, Mary, was a ready convert to the charms of a Norwegian Christmas. "I taught her to make *krumkake* before we were married," recalls Stephen, who learned the art in Norway.

"The tree trimming and hall decking take three days, and we start the day after Thanksgiving," says Mary. "We each have ornaments from our grandmothers and lots of personal treasures from friends and from our trips. After that I start baking." Another special cookie is *kringle,* a soft dough looped into pretzel shape. Dozens of these and other sweets keep fresh in tins until the family begins enter-

taining early in December. The table is always set with linen, silver, flowers, and candles—beautifully reflecting memories of Christmas in Norway.

The Knutsons' home provides a welcome setting for the festivities. Stephen, an architect specializing in restoring vintage homes, admires the Georgian revival style of the apartment, the work of Chicago architect Robert DeGolyer.

"Suburban apartments had a distinct character—elegant and spacious—necessary to lure affluent people out of their homes," Stephen notes.

The floor plan of the Knutsons' apartment is an excellent example. Wide archways both separate and connect the entrance hall, the living room, and the dining room with its handsome fireplace mantel and bay of four wide windows, which reach to the top of the 9-foot ceiling. A step through another living room archway is a sun porch. The overall effect is of both openness and formality. "The proportions are perfect," Stephen says. "The scale is superb."

Mary adds, "It's great for entertaining, which is what we love to do."

When it comes to furnishings, "I love the heartiness and richness of Victorian pieces," says Stephen. "They're big and fat and comfortable." He's not similarly enamored of the Victorian tendency toward deep colors ("dull" to Stephen) and heavy draping. He prefers vibrant colors and an open, airy interior.

"We've taken the Victorian motif and abstracted it," says Stephen, who painted his walls red and his woodwork white.

"We have no lace curtains or velvet draperies, fringe or doilies, or heavy carpets," Mary explains. The windows have been left bare, the furniture is upholstered in plain white, bright plaid, and a fresh, super-size primrose pattern. The floors are gleaming oak.

Cranberry walls and a collection of Blue Willow china overlook a dining table topped with topiaries handmade by Stephen, right. The 1860s ballroom chairs color-match the burled yew table.

"We loved the furniture. We loved the apartment," Stephen says. "It had to go together. When you have things you like, you find a place for them." In this case, the right place was dictated by adhering, "rather rigidly," says Stephen, to the Georgian revival style of symmetry and balance in furniture arrangement.

Many pieces are from local house sales, including a handsome, circa-1850 rosewood piano. Like much of the Knutsons' furniture, the round walnut table and Gay Nineties parlor chair are auction finds.

The couple have also added to the collection of Blue Willow earthenware that was started for them by Stephen's mother, Margaret, as a wedding gift. Hundreds of pieces from more than 20 companies now are displayed in cabinets and on walls and tabletops throughout the apartment. "Grouped, they give the impact of a single object," points out Mary. "It's not formal. That's why we like it, why it works here."

Similarly informal are the varied objects decorated with exuberant rosemaling. Literally "rose painting," this stylized folk art developed in the Norwegian countryside centuries ago to decorate churches, homes, furniture, and household objects. Rosemaling is characterized by bold, flowing strokes of rich reds, blues, greens, and golds.

The apartment is at its festive best at Christmastime, when the Knutson family gather in Chicago to celebrate their Norwegian heritage. "Aunt Evelyn and Uncle Richie always have the most remarkable party," Stephen says. "It's the Sunday before Christmas. There's goose and herring and krumkake, of course, and presents for all. It's something like the Christmas in Norway." Because the hosts live in Chicago, the out-of-town contingent of the family adjourns to the Knutsons' apartment

for what Stephen happily calls a slumber party. Then all gather again on Christmas Eve at the Knutson family farm in Millbrook, Illinois, to resume the seasonal festivities.

"That's what I love about Christmas," Stephen muses. "Excess and abundance!" A similar outlook on furnishing explains something of the charm of the Knutsons' bright apartment in all seasons. "Our home is more personal . . . domestic . . . friendly," says the architect, "because we brought in the Victorian furniture, the earthenware, the rosemaling."

Adds Mary, "We enjoy beauty, all kinds. It's so good to live with things that give us some relationship to the past." □

Blue and white, a color scheme provided by the china collection in much of the rest of the apartment, becomes the dominant theme in the Knutsons' master bedroom, opposite.

A walnut Victorian china cabinet serves as a dresser, top left. Its toile-valanced glass doors balance the weight and design of the draperies on the master bedroom's opposite wall.

French wallpaper and an Eastlake-style Victorian dresser add elegance to the master bath, bottom. Garlands and an antique Norwegian drinking horn filled with holly serve as reminders of the holiday season.

The *Spirit* Of a St. Louis *Christmas*

BY SUSAN DAVIDSON

PRODUCED BY MARY ANNE THOMSON • PHOTOGRAPHY BY WILLIAM HOPKINS

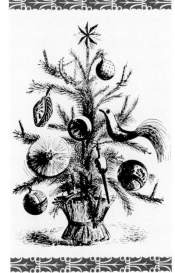

*C*HOIRS OF
ANGELIC TREASURES
GATHER THROUGHOUT
THE HOME OF
KEN MIESNER AND
JOHN SULLIVAN,
HELPING THEM
BEHOLD THE WARMTH
AND WONDER
OF THE SEASON.

*R*ed as Santa's suit, the
front door to Ken Miesner
and John Sullivan's St. Louis
home is always open to
holiday visitors, opposite.
Inside, Staffordshire dogs and
figures gather, left, while
John readies glasses of cheer.

*Where angels do not tread in this home, animals
and flowers rush in. In the living room at right, for example, puppy
pillows, horsey accents, an animal-print stool,
and orchids give Christmas an exotic twist. Tea, cookies, and a
blazing fire, below, welcome guests.*

All through the St. Louis home of Ken Miesner and John Sullivan, angels gather in bands, hosts, and choirs. Atop robust firs festooned with beads and silk of burnished gold, they gaze down like wise saints. They alight upon a dazzling crèche to behold with wonder the miracle of the Nativity. Or, like rarefied moths before a flame, they are found blithely fluttering amid the greenery encircling a Provence chandelier.

"We really love the angels," says John. "They are like old friends when we pull them out each year at Christmastime."

Ken and John impart the warmth, mystery, and surprise of the season to all they touch at home and at work. As the owners of Ken Miesner's, a floral and home accessories shop, they prepare for Christmas again and again in a frenzied rush to bedeck their clients' mantels, spiral staircases, front doors, and trees with fresh plants, silky ribbons, and sparkling glass and silver.

"We never lose sight of the owner," says Ken. "We always try to personalize our decorating. We'll use clients' things but update them, freshen them, to give a new look. It just makes the home special."

Despite the madcap business pace, Ken and John always find time to decorate their own home for the season. "We work like maniacs at the shop and have practically no personal

*KEN AND JOHN
ARE VIRTUOSOS AT
IMPARTING THE
WARMTH, MYSTERY,
AND SURPRISE
OF THE CHRISTMAS
SEASON TO ALL
THEY TOUCH.*

Fresh ivy and a collection of jovial Santas adorn the 19th-century French marble mantel **opposite.** *An eclectic mix of seating pieces and an old Oriental rug contribute to the English-country style in the living room.*

Sponged walls and furnishings in the dining room
left *add up to a good-as-gold holiday setting. On the second-floor stair*
landing below, *an 18th-century clock keeps perfect time,*
and an English tea table holds a favorite statue—an 18th-century
French figure of the Madonna and Child.

life," John says, "but Christmas is a magical, special time for us. After decorating for everyone else, I don't think it would be fair not to decorate for ourselves. I'd feel like we cheated."

Not surprisingly, Ken and John's home is very much a reflection of their business, a beguiling blend of the sophisticated and naive all heightened and intensified by the magical ornamentation and imagery of Christmas. Many of their antiques and accessories, such as needlepoint pillows, oil paintings, and Staffordshire dogs, are found by scouring the English countryside—"all the shires," says John. "We live with what we sell, and we love what we sell. We always buy things with ourselves in mind. We realize that

THE HOME'S BEGUILING BLEND OF THE NAIVE AND SOPHISTICATED IS HEIGHTENED BY THE MAGICAL IMAGERY OF THE HOLIDAYS.

we are in business and can't take everything home, although it may look like we are trying."

The sweet, smoky scent from dozens of candles pervades the two-story house and enhances the evocative spell of the holidays. John always scatters big bowls of fresh fruit and plates heaped with pomanders throughout the house, because the smells of Christmas are what he remembers best about growing up. "When I was a kid," he says, "we'd go to my grandparents on Christmas Eve to help put up the tree. Grandpa spread a big sheet under the tree and filled it with apples and oranges. The smell of bruised needles and fresh fruit has stayed with me all these years and reminds me of Christmas."

185

Made of canvas stretched across a barrel-shape wood frame, the 19th-century crèche opposite fills the window seat in the library. Ken and John rescued the niche from an antiques shop, but they believe it may have once served duty in a Catholic church.

Competing with the fragrant pomander balls and bowls of fresh fruit are a potpourri of fresh flowers and plants. A wreath of greens and wind-whipped wire ribbon decks the front door, where merrily jangling sleigh bells herald the arrival of guests. Boxwood and pine boughs, plucked from the backyard garden and fashioned into more wreaths, hang in the windows. Paper-whites and full-blown roses in pinks and crimsons fill the home with sweet scents and flashes of color. Feathery wisps of hemlock entwine the Provence chandelier in the dining room.

It never really seems like Christmas, however, until work begins trimming the tree. For good measure, there are two trees, one in the living room nuzzled against the stairs, and a second one in one of the upstairs bedrooms.

The trees, which hark back to old-fashioned Victorian excess, are decorated with

The detailed arms and stretchers of the Jacobean chair top left, known as the Barley twist, repeat the decoration found on the oak secretary, filled with Staffordshire dogs inside and out. Ken and John's favorite flowers, lilies, are represented in the form of a botanical print in this corner of the library.

A collection of carved wood bears, along with a Victorian Era stag-horn table and baronial needlepoint armchair, holds court in another corner of the library at left. Bern bears, as they are called, are a symbol of the Swiss capital. Ken, above, and John take time to enjoy their design and gardening books.

187

a pleasing jumble of ornaments both antique and new. Branches moan under the weight of jolly St. Nicks, silvery icicles, nostalgic candy cornucopias, fuzzy antique sheep, glittering glass balls, and, of course, angels.

"Many of the ornaments are things people have given us over the years," Ken says. "It's nice to bring them out and have those memories and think of those people, too." John adds: "I put special angels on one tree for my nieces."

When the last glass parasols and smiling Santas have been hung and the tinsel and beads strung just so, a trip is made to the basement to unearth an old crèche, which through some enchanted sleight-of-hand is transformed into a spellbinding Nativity scene.

Discovered years ago in an antiques shop, the 19th-century niche, composed of canvas stretched across a barrel-shape wooden frame, stands nearly 4 feet high and fills the window seat in the library. Set against a background of sapphire sky and glinting rays of golden light is Christ, surrounded by the seven archangels.

"It makes a wonderful crèche," says Ken. "It's something quite different."

In one sense, decorating the niche is a dress rehearsal for a grander event. Every Christmas Eve for the past 18 years, it has been Ken's great pleasure to shower majestic St. Louis Cathedral with all the bright blooms of the season.

"It's a wonderful feeling to be climbing around that Byzantine building, putting poinsettias around the statues with the organist rehearsing," Ken says. "It really gets you in the Christmas spirit." □

Index

Porches, 12–13, 18, 71, 79.
    See also Terraces
    back, 79, 85
    converting, 114
    enclosed, 111, 158
    front, 26
    sun, 50
Pot racks, 163
Pottery, 72

Q–S

Queen Anne
    chairs, 110, 116–117
    tables, 59,
Quilts, 12, 121, 142–143, 188
Rag rugs, 12–13
Ranch-style homes, 28–36, 124–134
Rockers, Shaker, 145
Rococo, American, 18
Roofs, vaulted, 46
Rosemaling, 171, 172, 173
Rugs
    Aubusson, 32–33
    dhurrie, 122
    kilim, 160–161
    needlepoint, 141
    Oriental, 52, 60, 114, 116–117,
        182–183
    rag, 12–13
    serape, 89
    sisal, 111
    tribal, 90
Rumford fireplaces, 66
Saltbox homes, 38–49
Screens
    fireplace, 98
    folding, 8, 28, 188
Sculptures, 20
Seating, angled, 141
Secretaries, 35, 43, 92, 187
Settees, 20. *See also* Sofas
Shaker rockers, 145
Shelves, 91, 142
Sideboards, 150
Signs, 138
Sinks, 24
Sitting rooms, 123, 140–141.
    See also Living rooms
Skylights, 160–161

Slipcovers, 141
Snuff bottles, 9
Sofas, 80, 89, 103, 114, 128–129
Southwestern furnishings, 124–134
Staffordshire figures, 178, 187
Staircases, 88, 109
Statues, 98, 185
    animal, 40, 43, 94, 150, 151, 159,
        178, 187
    bronze, 9, 11, 21
    Napoleon, 48
Stereo equipment, concealing, 16
Sterling boxes, 88
Stools, 55, 133
Storage boxes, 145
Studies, 11, 83, 130. *See also*
    Libraries
Stuffed animals, 188

T–Z

Table runners, 32–33
Tables
    Connecticut Queen Anne, 59
    baker's, 15
    breakfast, 66
    burled yew, 174–175
    butterfly-top, 62
    coffee, 80, 89, 129
    corner, 80
    country French dining, 144
    dining, 14, 23, 72–73, 82, 91,
        97, 110,
    drop-leaf, 60, 116–117
    end, 30, 141
    entry, 88
    farm, 132
    gateleg, 122
    harvest, 138
    kitchen, 25
    side, 60
    sofa, 129
    stag-horn, 187
    tavern, 122
    tea, 114, 185
    Thonet, 36
    tole, 11
    Victorian, 168–169
Tassels, 152
Teapots, 61
Teddy bears, 188

Televisions, concealing, 16, 130
Terraces, 47, 75, 118, 119. *See also*
    Porches
Tile, 25, 36, 154–155
Topiaries, 99, 175
Tortoiseshell, 43
Toy horses, 127, 138. *See also*
    Animals
Trunks, 17, 145
Upholstery
    Chinese-patterned, 54
    chintz, 12–13
    mattress ticking, 46
Vases, 21
Victorian
    furnishings, 168–169, 177
    homes, 18–26, 102–111
Walks, 79, 100, 113
Wall coverings
    crackle, 69
    fabric, 121
    hand-painted, 123
Walls
    sponged, 184
    upholstered, 24, 49
Wardrobes, 16, 53, 103, 163
Wedgewood, 61
Wells, 113
Wicker, 12, 50, 85, 111
Wildflowers, 138. *See also*
    Gardens
Window treatments, 35, 53, 57,
        60, 65, 142
    balloon shades, 91
    floral-print, 73
    swag and jabot, 68, 90 97
    valances, 33, 99, 177
Woodwork, pickled, 40